AN ADMIRABLE POINT

A BRIEF HISTORY OF
THE EXCLAMATION MARK!

FLORENCE HAZRAT

BOSTON

GODINE

2023

Published in 2023 by
GODINE
Boston, Massachusetts

First published in Great Britain by Profile Books, Ltd. in 2022.

LIBRARY OF CONGRESS CATALOGING-IN-PUBLICATION DATA
Names: Hazrat, Florence, author.
Title: An admirable point : a brief history of [!] / Florence Hazrat.
Description: Boston : Godine, 2023.
Identifiers: LCCN 2022038098 (print) | LCCN 2022038099 (ebook) | ISBN
    9781567927870 (paperback) | ISBN 9781567927887 (ebook)
Subjects: LCSH: Exclamation point--History.
Classification: LCC P301.5.P86 H39 2023 (print) | LCC P301.5.P86 (ebook)
    | DDC 411/.7--dc23/eng/20220917
LC record available at https://lccn.loc.gov/2022038098
LC ebook record available at https://lccn.loc.gov/2022038099

First Printing, 2023
Printed in the United States of America

This book is dedicated to those who give attention to small things. And to Alpoleio, who invented a new mark of punctuation to make us wonder and admire more – if possible with abandon!

Editor's Note

This first U.S. edition of *An Admirable Point* retains the author's U.K. spelling, punctuation, formatting, and terminology so as not to water down the text's unique vernacular. This means, amongst other things, that what is referred to in the U.S. as the *exclamation point* is here called the *exclamation mark*, *periods* are *full stops*, and *parentheses* are *brackets*.

CONTENTS

!

INTRODUCTION

The spiked delights of !

On 21 January 1788, a triplet of !!!s nearly brought down the project of the United States of America before it got off the ground. The *Boston Gazette* printed an attention-commanding headline in capital letters followed by three hysterical exclamation marks, inflaming public concerns about the future of the fledgling nation: 'BRIBERY AND CORRUPTION!!!', the title read. Below, readers were told that the 'most diabolical plan is on foot to corrupt the members of the Convention, who oppose the adoption of the New Constitution'. Massachusetts politicians were being offered 'large sums of money' from a 'neighbouring State' to put aside their concerns about the most crucial document of the young country, the Constitution.

Although the American Constitution was born in an inspired four-month spell, it needed ratification in at least nine of the thirteen states. This process was arduous, involving the local assemblies in heated debates of the very same issues over which the states had split from their mother country: taxation, overseeing commerce, the distribution of legal and executive powers, personal liberties. By January 1788, five states had ratified, but the process had stalled in Massachusetts. This was fertile ground in which to sow doubt, and the *Gazette*'s article duly fanned the flames of unrest and mistrust. The power of those !!!s was so great in whipping up public emotion that George Washington had to step in. He sent word to the state's convention that they absolutely must agree to the Constitution, but that there could be a set of amendments to address the delegates' reservations. These amendments would become the Bill of Rights, enshrining the individual's rights in relation to the government in the heart of American political identity.

The Massachusetts convention then approved the proposed Constitution and the United States of America was born. All thanks to a string of exclamation marks.

— !!! —

! makes us cry out – so much so that it's been called the screamer, the slammer, the bang, the gasper, and the shriek. It's bubbly and exuberant, an emotional amplifier whose flamboyantly dramatic gesture lets the reader know: *here be feelings!* As such, ! has received undue amounts of flak: in 2016, the UK Department of Education issued a new guideline for primary school learners that caused public outcry: teachers would be tasked with downgrading pupils who used what was seen as an excessive number of exclamation marks. An ! should only follow a sentence starting with 'how' or 'what' (as in 'How silly!' and 'What nonsense!'). Public and media alike protested at what they saw as dictatorial language policing, although the government was of course just trying to protect the young citizens from what the urban dictionary calls 'bangorrhea'.

It's not only conservative government agents who dislike !. Many writers have warned against using the mark, claiming it provides cheap emphasis. F. Scott Fitzgerald declared that exclamation marks are like laughing at your own jokes; Terry Pratchett had a character in *Discworld* say multiple !!!s are a 'sure sign of a diseased mind' (five being a 'sign of someone wearing his underpants on his head'). ! is all things 'too': too noisy, too attention-grabbing, too powerful, too present. Journalist Philip Cowell sneers at its confident self-referential *thereness*, calling it 'the selfie of grammar'. There's a blog called 'Excessive Exclamation' that posts photos sent by geeks upset by the inflationary intrusion of !, !!! or even !!!!!!!!!!! into the public sphere.

So, is the exclamation mark only for the irrational, the deranged and Gen Z self-display addicts? Is it a hot and messy extra dish that we don't really need at the already plentiful banquet of language? If so, it is astonishing that it exists in nearly every language from Persian to Mandarin. It's also surprising for how many likely and unlikely cultural functions we have enlisted !. Its concise and expressive ta-da!-quality provided a shortcut for Victor Hugo's publisher, who, in answer to the author's anxious telegrammed '?' concerning the sales of *Les Misérables*, wired back a triumphant '!'. German writer Christian Morgenstern casts an exclamation mark as an emphatic preacher in his 'Realm of Punctuation', a humorous poem on the murder of semicolons.

A straight downwards stroke, a crisp dot underneath: the exclamation mark packs a punch, with its uniquely assertive shape. In 2010, the American children's TV show *The Electric Company* had none other than hip-hop legend LL Cool J rap different punctuation rules while meeting outsized animated versions of each individual mark. The first one popping out behind him, and growing

to twice the singer's height, was the exclamation mark, its imposing shape exuding a boss-like presence. The German version of the literary detective trio 'The Three Investigators' is called *Die drei ???* ('The Three ???'); the trio ask question after question until they have cracked even the toughest secret. In 2006, the German publisher introduced the (overdue) female counterpart, *Die drei !!!*, neatly capitalising on the vertical aspect of the punctuation in its logo.

—!!!—

If any punctuation mark has the potential to look like a phallus, it must be !. Beloved French humorist Pierre Desproges comically admonishes us to avoid 'such facile punctuation whose cocky one-balled design can only hurt modesty'. Perhaps that's why Henry Miller, a pioneer of sexually explicit literature, cautioned over-eager erotica writers: 'Keep your exclamation marks under control!'. There may be a lot going on in the narrative, but ! should not be the source of the excitement. One of the greatest female entertainers of the first half of the twentieth century (and also one of the highest-paid women in the world at the time), French cabaret artist Mistinguett, explained that 'a kiss can be a comma, a question mark, or an exclamation mark.' The !-ed kiss is certainly not a peck on the cheek.

The exclamation mark (and its shape) also has a certain shock value: ! signifies high alert and protest. These made it an effective tool for representatives of the European Parliament who, in a Strasbourg session in 2013, expressed their discontent with Hungary's authoritarian changes to its constitution with a silent sea of !!!s.

Hungary's assault on democracy provokes the European Parliament.

! keeps us on our toes, and when we see it we know something noteworthy is going on, quite possibly something dangerous or provocative. In the lists used by professional Scrabble players, an exclamation mark denotes a word that is considered offensive but may be played in some, if not all, circumstances. In 1978, the Merriam-Webster dictionary published the first Scrabble list, but later encountered criticism regarding its inclusion of racial and sexual slurs as well as rather more innocent scatological terms. Under pressure from various interested parties, from anti-defamation leagues to Scrabble player associations, the dictionary publisher and the toy maker Mattel have produced revised lists that reflect the socio-linguistic sensitivities of the moment. Currently forbidden are insults such as LEZ, but also words living on the edge of politeness, such as FARTED, BOOBIE and PISSED (although FUCK seems to have been spared). Mattel's vice-president Ray Adler reflects that 'in Scrabble – as in life – the words you choose matter'. And so does the punctuation.

There's something about the exclamation mark that makes us move. With three simple black lines, motivational author James Victore transforms a splurge of shouting orange into a determined matchstick figure, encouraging us to 'Just start' instead of overthinking a project, letting it stall before it has even lifted off.

The exclamation mark generates excitement, and also transmits it. Folklore has it that the twelfth-century German bishop Johannes Fugger, travelling to Rome for the inauguration of the Holy Roman Emperor, sent his prelate ahead in order to identify the inns with the best

Just start! James Victore's motivational exclamation mark.

wines. The prelate would mark the doors of the approved inns with a chalked Latin 'est' ('there is', as in 'there is good wine'). Arriving in the village of Montefiascone, the prelate found such amazingly delicious wine that he exclaimed on the door 'est! est!! est!!!'. The bishop himself was so taken with the stuff that he abandoned his trip although barely sixty miles away from Rome, and spent the rest of his life quaffing Montefiascone wine with his prelate. The story is a legend (! was invented hundreds of years later), but the wine's reputation stuck. Today, you can still buy *Est! Est!! Est!!!* white wine, although it leaves connoisseurs rather less ecstatic than Fugger's sidekick.

Beware those not excited enough! In a notable scene between Elaine (the female lead character from *Seinfeld*) and her then-boyfriend Jake, Elaine notices the glaring absence of ! at the end of a note Jake had taken for her from a friend who'd called to say she'd had a baby. Elaine wonders if such punctuational neglect might indicate a lack of emotional interest in her life (although she never tells her boyfriend as much). Rapidly escalating, the exclamation mark conflict leads to a hot-headed break-up, with Jake storming out of the apartment, shouting at Elaine to go ahead and put an air-sliced !-gesticulation on his parting statement: 'I'm leaving!'.

There's a small but select strand of punctuation jokes in TV comedy: in the US version of *The Office*, for example, Jim and Dwight are planning a birthday party for their colleague Kelly, and getting everything wrong, including the poster. Dwight puts up a plain black-and-white 'IT IS YOUR BIRTHDAY.' sign, eliciting exasperation from Jim, who believes an affectionate exclamation mark is the least they could do for their co-worker. 'It's a statement of fact,' Dwight counters: 'This is more professional. It's not like she discovered a cure for cancer.'

— !!! —

You don't have to patent a ground-breaking medical innovation in order to ride the wave of !. Plenty of bands, brands and shows know the difference between a dot and a dash: while singer P!NK explodes the power of ! in mid-name, Yahoo!, *Jeopardy!*, *Moulin Rouge!* and *Mamma Mia!* jump off the exclamation mark springboard. German fashion designer Wolfgang Joop even wanted to

copyright the punctuation of his logo JOOP!, embroiling himself in a three-year lawsuit with the European trademark office, which eventually dismissed his claim. ! belongs to everyone. There's a sense of declarativeness in !, a sense of urgency which pins the reader onto the page of now. Jazz musician Jackie McLean doubles that hurry by tilting the orientation of typeface on the cover of his 1964 album, letting ! run wildly across line after line after line.

Half a century later, ! can still ruffle our feathers when we see it in a close cluster of brothers and sisters. In 2010, punk rock collective Bomb the Music Industry! released an album under the catchy title *Adults!!!: Smart!!! Shithammered!!! And Excited by Nothing!!!!!!!*. That's seven marks at the end. Nothing gets us as excited as !. And how does one pronounce a free-falling exclamation?

Low Wham transformed!

American rock band **!!!** is happy to be known as the only slightly more performable Chk Chk Chk.

! detonates on the page and our ears, and also in our mouths: the International Phonetic Alphabet employs '!' to indicate the placement of the tongue on the gum's ridge just behind the upper teeth, producing a click sound found in several Khoisan languages in south-western Africa such as '!Kung'. Most sign languages have punctuation mark hand movements to mimic written shapes when finger-spelling, but (as in the spoken version of the language) punctuation's job in signed speech is done through the face, postures and gestures.

The most famous musical mark of exclamation is in the name of eternal Christmas-song artistes Wham!, created

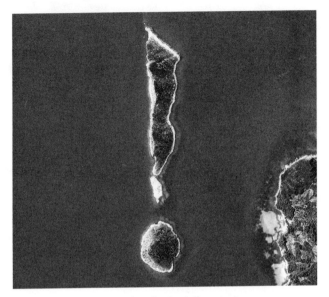

Yılan and Siçam, punctuating the Anatolian coast.

by schoolfriends George Michael and Andrew Ridgeley. Reflecting on their trademark punctuation, Ridgeley explained that their sound of comic book collision, followed by a cheeky !, represented the duo's 'energy' and 'friendship', a 'snappy, immediate, fun and boisterous' name you wouldn't forget. Just in time for Christmas 2020, a fan turned the street sign for the village of 'Low Wham' in the north of England to 'Last Christmas Wham!'. (The manipulated sign was still there the very next day).

There are exclamation marks on signs, and there is ! in the wild. The small Turkish islands of Yılan and Siçam, seen together from the sky, create a near-perfect exclamation mark, just off the south-west coast of Antalya region. The long slender island Yılan means 'snake', the circular foot Siçam 'mouse', lying curled under the menacing head of its punctuation counterpart.

A curious phenomenon of ! in geography occurs in some place names. The Devon resort of Westward Ho! is a case in point, offering its exclamation mark as a gimmick to attract tourists (the name, including the !, comes from the title of a novel by Charles Kingsley). But it's the Québecois Saint-Louis-du-Ha! Ha! which became winner of the 2017 Guinness World Record for the town with the most exclamation marks in its name. Quite how the little Canadian town came by its name is unclear – perhaps the founding missionaries had exclaimed in surprise, when struck with the unexpected impasse of a lake.

At Princeton University, ! was employed as a path specification for early forms of email. Imitating neural connections that chunk information to encode and transmit it economically, a typical proto-email address looked like Princeton!maths!Bob. The message would go from the centre at Princeton to the maths server, and then to department member Bob; the exclamation mark represented each intersection. When mathematicians are having fun, they come up with factorials signalled by ! and so-called 'shriek maps' in which exceptional functors are marked with a !. In chess notation, an exceptional move is marked with !! in transcriptions; a plain ! denotes a strong move; !? signifies interesting but risky; while ?! signifies dubious.

! crops up everywhere in our daily lives, from poetry, museums and high-brow scholarship to ads, tweets and pop culture. The versatile exclamation mark effortlessly permeates social barriers, adapting to just about any and every occasion and context. It's a chameleon whose ability to affect the mood in those encountering it is both welcome and worrisome. Intrepid fans and inveterate opponents know: ! skilfully inspires strong feelings in us readers, even as it boldly registers those feelings from the author on the written page. The exclamation mark sneaks into our brains and bodies, and it makes us nervous – as it should.

— !!! —

An Admirable Point sets out to reclaim the exclamation mark from its much maligned and misunderstood place at the bottom of the punctuation hierarchy. It argues that there is a lot of sense in flagging up textual shouting (think of the zoological 'Duck' versus the life-saving 'Duck!'), and it examines a much more nuanced understanding of the workings of ! in sentences, and our minds. It explores how ! came into existence some six hundred years ago, and will make a case for why it makes sense to cling onto it. We'll uncover the many ways in which ! has left its mark on art, literature, pop culture and just about any sphere of human activity.

The turncoat exclamation mark accommodates meaning beyond text, and voraciously claims new functions in unexpected fields. As such, ! is vulnerable to misuse; its controversial charisma carries it into the shady places of mass manipulation as chapters on politics, advertising, cognitive science and digital communication will probe.

An Admirable Point is a proclamation of unapologetic enthusiasm for what Princeton literature professor Lee

Clarke Mitchell calls the 'spiked delights' of !. It encourages us to pay attention, to look closely, to pause and think. It makes supposedly transparent and self-effacing punctuation visible, so that its role in communication can be apprehended. When 280-character tweets can influence elections, chart pandemics and shift markets, it is crucial to understand the promises and pitfalls of letters, fonts, emojis and punctuation marks, most of all the paradoxical !!!.

In his 1611 English–French dictionary, Randle Cotgrave defined ! as 'the point of admiration (and detestation)'. The parenthesis, smuggled into an otherwise straightforward definition, shows how the exclamation mark is both definite and hard to define. It can be several things at the same time, and sometimes contradictory ones – wonder as well as disgust. It's slippery, flying from the highs to the lows on the spectrum of human emotion. The wayward ambiguity of ! has always worried us. Perhaps because the exclamation mark reached outside of its paper habitat, and into our bodies, it is an affective sign, and it asks for an affective reaction from us. Fear, anger, surprise, joy – suddenly, abstract letters become alive, magicked into feeling by the dot and the bar hovering just above. ! has agency over us. This book is an invitation to let it have it.

CHAPTER ONE

A very pathetical point
! through the ages

Dishwashers, cars, mobile phones. How often do we stop and think about the objects we use every day that make our life significantly easier? And not just objects, but social rituals like Christmas or handshakes, and indeed writing itself, a seven-thousand-year-old accomplishment we have inherited from generation after generation. All of those things, all of those habits and intellectual achievements, at first did not exist, and had to be invented at some point, but most of us will take them for granted. We take it for granted that we tame our thoughts into a bunch of silent arbitrary squiggles squeezed into line on a piece of paper or a screen, and that those same squiggles can come to life again in someone else's thought or throat at the other end of the world, or in the distant unknowable future.

And it's not only letters themselves that have a history, but also those inky marks dotted here and there between

wayward words, attempting (but not always) to orchestrate their anarchic tendencies. The ancient Greeks and
Romans, for example, understood writing as a record of
speech, not a separate manifestation of language.
Therefore, it didn't occur to them to put spaces between
individual words likesowhichmakesreadingrathercumber
someandslow. This certainly saves space (especially
useful if you have to laboriously chisel each letter into
marble), but it was counter-productive for inexperienced
Greek or Latin readers who had no idea where a word
ended and another started, let alone one of those elabo-
rately convoluted sentences. Ancient librarians, teachers
and learners developed a system of signs to help understand the anatomy of sentences, and to know where to
stop for breath.

Versions of the comma, colon and the full stop (plus
spaces between the words for increased clarity) became
crutches for reading and writing, serving just fine for nearly
a thousand years. From the fifth to the thirteenth centuries,
the Church mostly took care of the business of writing,
which resulted in a lack of experimentation and
development. From around the thirteenth century onwards,
however, Italian city states and universities started to
develop, contesting the Church's right to the written word.
Reading and writing became available for activities other
than theology, for trade, diplomacy, even love poetry. As
textual traffic increased, three marks of punctuation were
no longer enough to carry the burden of communication:
new signs were necessary to navigate the subtleties of
writing. The question mark and the exclamation mark

joined the ranks of punctuation points, helping readers identify the tone of a sentence at first glance.

While the question mark migrated into worldly writing outside the monasteries (where it served the musical purpose of lifting the voice in chanting), the exclamation mark was a stroke of genius from one man who, sometime in the mid-fourteenth century, was seized with the desire to propose a wholly novel sign. In his treatise *The Art of Punctuating*, Italian scholar and poet Iacopo Alpoleio da Urbisaglia muses: 'seeing that the exclamatory or admirative sentences were pronounced in the same way as continuing or interrogative discourse, I acquired the habit of pointing the end of such sentences by means of a clear point, and a comma placed to the side above that same point'. A sort of full stop with a comma or apostrophe hovering to its right. A cheeky little textual earring dangling from the top of the line.

The exclamation mark was a rebel even at its birth. It would take another half-century, however, and the imaginative effort of another punctuation fan, to register the first visual form of the exclamation mark. In 1399, the Florentine lawyer and politician Coluccio Salutati transformed Alpoleio's words into the ! we know today, in his text *De nobilitate legum et medicinae* (1399). Picking a

Coluccio Salutati introduces the exclamation mark (near the end of line 2) in his *De nobilitate legum et medicinae*, 1399.

humorous bone with medical doctors, Coluccio contends that medicine is not knowledge but conjecture, unlike the law. Replying to Bernhardinus Florentinus, who had praised medicine, Salutati bursts into mock-emotion: 'I earnestly urge you and other doctors, please reply to me!'. The same manuscript also contains the first brackets, sectioning off additional matter within the sentence. Although the text was noted down or copied from drafts by Coluccio's secretary, it shows his own handwritten changes, including punctuation marks wedged between the narrow string of words.

Such attention to the minutiae of language was a hallmark of a new love for words, their sound, their style. Coluccio spearheaded what we now call humanism, the Renaissance zeitgeist that venerated the culture and the stories of ancient Greece and Rome, their gracefully poised sentences and their celebration of the ideal man as persuasive orator. Imitating the ancients in all things except their pagan religion, writers of the Renaissance sought to import this oratorical ideal from Classical Athens and Rome into the pages of their letters of diplomacy, trade and scholarly disputes.

Attempting to control how their readers would understand their written words, humanists invented and formalised more and more signs of punctuation, such as the semicolon, the apostrophe, the ellipsis (...), various kinds of brackets (round, curly and angular), the dash, the hyphen and quotation marks. Our current punctuation marks largely developed within a mere two hundred years between 1400 and 1600, remaining pretty much unchanged since and sharing an enormous amount of textual duty between them, as workhorses of the written word, unthanked but also uncontested – at least until very recently, when the internet hijacked their ability to separate sentences, and emojis began to compete with punctuation's skill in conveying and creating emotions.

Back then, of course, there was no such thing as a redcheeked smiley, or eggplant, or sheepish monkey-face to thread feelings into one's text (it's hard to imagine the likes of Luther or Erasmus sending prayerhands). Instead, writers harnessed punctuation to capture and evoke emotion, well aware that the naked content of words without the dress of feelings would have a hard time convincing anyone. It's no surprise, then, that Alpoleio, Coluccio and company engineered an effectively affective new sign that

Apple

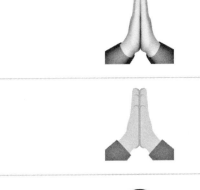

Google

Microsoft

Prayer hand emojis from the big tech companies.

Coluccio Salutati – scholar, humanist, bibliophile ... and exclamation mark pioneer.

embodied the voice and feeling of the speaker in the hope that it would work its magic within the reader, too.

Coluccio was an influential writer and literary patron, and his exclamation mark and brackets began to trickle into other texts by other writers. But they might have drifted into oblivion had they not been picked up by the first printers, who in the fifteenth century established shops in Mainz and Frankfurt, and shortly after in Basel, Lyon, Venice and other cities. The technological advances of the printing press enabled the fast duplication of texts that were carried into all corners of early modern Europe. Standard versions of books started to appear, from the Bible to schoolbooks; Julius Caesar's *Gallic Wars* was a favourite. But it was not only the words that became uniform: the appearance of the page also crystallised through the work and experimentation of a few master printers. Punctuation marks were not exempt, and thus the now-upright form of ! entered all European languages.

Presence, however, does not mean universal use, nor comprehension. The French scholar and writer Rabelais would have benefited from some !s in his scatological tales of gluttonous giants producing huge amounts of farts and piles of poo. Telling of the pregnant lady giant who has devoured buckets of tripe and wine in spite of warnings that she will burst, the narrator wryly comments: 'O, the beautiful faecal matter that's blowing up inside of her!' Such inflation certainly deserves that astonished !, but it remains one of the few in Rabelais's gigantic oeuvre. This particular exclamation mark appears in his own corrected copy of the 1542 edition, but is absent in many others before and after. The exclamation mark could have been the perfect point to encapsulate the excess of body, food, shit and hilarity Rabelais bounced off one another; yet ! was not well enough known and understood to truly impact readers in their experience of the tales.

Readers, writers and printers were certainly aware of the exclamation mark, but they weren't quite sure how to apply it, resulting in a wild lack of consistency from writer to writer (and even within individual texts). The growth and usage of punctuation marks was erratic at best and messy at worst, as was the development of European languages at the time.

The British Isles were far behind the continent in terms of paper and printing technology and know-how – but also progress with their native English (or Scots) as a language that could compete with the perceived richness and nuance of Latin as a medium of power at the court, chancery and universities. During the sixteenth and seventeenth centuries, English writers experimented and explored, inventing new words or borrowing them and Anglicising them more or less successfully. They also introduced and discarded new punctuation marks, and pushed for language reform. One such writer was the educator John Hart, who worried about inconsistent spelling, based on the vastly differing dialects of English, from Cornwall to Cumbria, and on the essentially medieval orthography of English, whose sounds had since moved on.

Writing in the 1550s and 1560s, Hart believed that 'vicious' spelling 'bringeth confusion and uncertainty in the reading', especially then where there was enough confusion and uncertainty in religious and political terms already. His proposals for a phonetic spelling reform didn't catch on, but he offers possibly the earliest mentions of ! in English. In his 1551 manuscript, *The Opening of the Unreasonable Writing of our English Tongue*, Hart calls !

'the wonderer', and deals with it together with its brother **?** ('the asker') because of their identical grammatical function of ending a sentence and offering direction on its tone. He recommends prefacing questions and exclamations with the two signs, because they 'tune the voice'. This anticipation of the Spanish practice of initial upside-down marks did not catch on, nor did many others of Hart's suggestions, although he did have an impact on the way scholars and educators thought about English grammar and spelling. If lexicographers were unsure quite how to use the mark, it's no surprise writers and printers alike struggled. What made matters worse was the close kinship between **!** and **?** in terms of rhetorical questions: is it more of a question, or an exclamation? Or is it both?!

Apart from the confusion over tone and style, very practical circumstances also came into play over the looks and effect of the exclamation mark. Until the Industrial Revolution, printing was a slow laborious craft that meant text would be read out to the typesetter (or skimmed by the setter), who would sit at a desk with two cases, containing boxes with the individual letters of the alphabet, punctuation marks and space signs. The typesetter would balance an oblong tray in one hand, filling it with the required type with the other, and then arrange the trays line by line in big frames. The frames would be bound tightly, inked and pressed onto sheets of paper, which were dried, folded, cut, stitched together and sold, or bound with sturdy covers before sitting on the stalls of booksellers.

Printing in the sixteenth and seventeenth centuries was expensive, because buying type and paper demanded

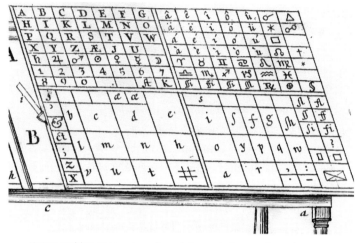

Upper and lower case type for printers – but no exclamation mark. From Joseph Moxon, *Mechanick exercises, or, The doctrine of handy-works: applied to the art of printing* (London: 1683).

considerable advance investment for uncertain returns. Printers bought type sets from a handful of foundries across Europe. Some sets included !, some didn't, as the mark was not yet established. Whether an exclamation mark could be used (if there was one in the manuscript) thus depended on the availability of type, although printers could (and did) help themselves by repurposing existing type, building an exclamation-tower from a dot and a comma much the same way as Alpoleio proposed. Whether ! was included in the type a printer owned also depended on the kinds of works they habitually produced: a printer of theology or natural sciences would not need type that contained markers of emotion like !. A printed play, on the other hand, or poetry, was a different textual creature altogether, necessitating emotive punctuation.

In the late seventeenth century, the printer Joseph Moxon released the first English instructional manual for printers, containing information on the craft, including woodcuts of type cases. Moxon was an educated tradesman who contributed to the advancement of science through printing maps and mathematical papers, as well as making globes and measuring instruments. As a member of the Royal Society and the king's own hydrographer, responsible for the survey of British rivers and lakes, Moxon was not in the business of producing emotive texts. As was to be expected, the cases in the image of his manual have no designated boxes for ! (unlike specially cut type for the signs of the zodiac, still part and parcel of Renaissance science).

By the middle of the eighteenth century, however, ! had become an accepted member of the punctuation family, and was included, for example, in John Smith's *The Printer's Grammar.*

ﬆ	[ ]	æ	œ	ç	'		s	( )	?	!	;	ﬂ	ff
& / ﬄ	b	c	d	e		i	f	f	g	ﬃ	ff	ﬀ
											ﬁ	ﬁ
j / H S.	l	m	n	h		o	y	p	q	w	*n*	*m*
z / x	v	u	t	*Spaces*		a	r	, / .	: / -			Qu.

Here it is! A designated exclamation mark box appears in the lower case box (top row) in John Smith's *The Printer's Grammar* (London: 1755).

So, when looking at a book from the Renaissance, we need to keep in mind the realities of how a text migrated from the unique handwritten pages of the author to the pile of neat obedient prints, remembering all the in-between stages that contain decision after decision: is this a **c** or an **r**? Shall we add some dashes to fill out the line? Do we even have enough !!!s left to have the character exclaim here? The final choices were made in the print shop, and motivated by expedience and educated guesswork. Few authors were involved enough in their works to stand on punctuation. Few, indeed, punctuated their manuscripts with more than the bare minimum: until the nineteenth century, punctuation was a matter of personal taste, as it still is today to some degree. A gentleman of the nobility could be found punctuating very little, and a poor scholar very much, according to their inclination. Some writers and printers tended to be more involved, others less so. Moxon himself complained of the 'carelessness of some good authors, and the ignorance of other authors', which has 'forced printers to introduce ... a task and duty incumbent on the compositor, namely to discern and amend the bad spelling and pointing of his copy'. He concludes 'it is necessary that a compositor be a good English scholar at least'.

Compositors and printers were more learned than many people, at least in matters of language, but that didn't save them from the disdain of a certain author who did care about the detail, and very much so. Ben Jonson, friend of Shakespeare, and fellow playwright and poet, griped about the printer of his 1631 complete works, John Beale, whom he called 'lewd' for 'loosing [his] points', and thus loosening his 'sense'. A considerable number of Jonson's manuscripts survive, and confirm him as a heavy punctuator, trying to control the meaning and rhythm of his lines, in apparent contrast to Shakespeare – at least, in as much as we can gather from the record. For, apart from a handful of signatures, the only substantial autograph we have of Shakespeare are three smudged pages of a play co-written with five other playwrights.

The play traces the life of Sir Thomas More, the much-loved counsellor and victim of King Henry VIII. It was revised several times, because it was deemed to be potentially inflammatory, with its portrayal of historical riots in

Shakespeare's smudged manuscript of his co-written play, *Sir Thomas More*, c.1601–4.

1517. Shakespeare's manuscript adds an emotive speech by More, quelling the violent protest against foreigners dwelling in London by asking for compassion for those who have to leave their home for a life in an unknown country. Even that was too much for the censor, and the play was never staged or printed until modern times.

Thomas More's speech is as stylish and stirring as we'd expect from Shakespeare, but we might not have thought the Bard would cross out his words quite so much, and use such sparse punctuation: there are only a few commas here and there, some full stops, and no question or exclamation marks at all, where we would insert them aplenty. One explanation may be that Shakespeare wrote fast, passed on his pages to the next collaborator and moved onto the next project. He was a writer for a rapidly changing market. Another is that he was writing a text for a play that was never intended to remain imprisoned on paper: during rehearsals, the actors themselves would decide where to pause, and how to emphasise the words, so there was no need to encode rhythm or tone into the silent skeleton of a play's words.

Much ink has been spilled over whether Shakespeare was involved in the printing of his works and, if so, to what degree. The most likely conclusion is that he was a careful and clever negotiator of the environments of both printed and live theatre, and was fully aware of what was needed to maximise financial reward and reputation. During Shakespeare's lifetime, some of his pieces were published individually, some several times, and in different versions. In 1623, seven years after his death, a group of publishers printed a collected edition, *Mr William Shakespeares Comedies, Histories & Tragedies*. This was an expensive and complex undertaking of 1,000 copies of a 900-page book, containing 36 plays printed on large-size paper, now called the First Folio. Eighteen of those plays had never before been printed, and may well have been lost had they not been included in the Folio. The base texts for the collection were probably a combination of existent printed plays, prompt books used in the theatre, working drafts and authorial manuscripts, all now lost, so the punctuation may be a mixture created by Shakespeare, the copyists and compositors. In 1975, theatre director Peter Hall scoffed at the Folio's commas and friends, calling it 'absurdly over-punctuated', and speculating that 'the first printers popped in some extra-punctuation', which they most probably did, if their author offered so little.

Scholars have pieced together how five or six compositors set the type for the book, one of them identified as the apprentice Ralph Crane. Each compositor had different spelling and punctuation skills and habits: Ralph, for

Within the Booke and Volume of my Braine,
Vnmixt with baſer matter; yes, yes, by Heauen :
Oh moſt pernicious woman !
Oh Villaine, Villaine, ſmiling damned Villaine !
My Tables, my Tables; meet it is I ſet it downe,
That one may ſmile, and ſmile and be a Villaine;
At leaſt I'm ſure it may be ſo in Denmarke ;
So Vnckle there you are : now to my word;

Hamlet soliloquises in the First Folio, 1623, with a rare outburst of exclamation marks.

example, loved parentheses. Nobody, it seems, was much of a fan of !, perhaps because grasp of its use was still so vague. Linguist David Crystal has counted just 350 exclamation marks in the Folio, an extremely small number for a book of its length, and a theatrical book at that, full of declamatory speeches and emotional outbursts. Of the 350 !s Crystal has spotted, 265 launch with 'Oh' or 'O', sometimes implying a desperate sigh or growl of anger, sometimes an address to an absent or present someone or something (think of Juliet's 'O, Romeo!', or 'O, moon!'). But hardly any 'O's or 'Oh's get their own !, nor do the other passionate phrases we deem to be exclamations today: Hamlet swears soberly 'by Heaven', but rails against his uncle ('Oh villain, villain, smiling damned villain!').

Does a change of punctuation make any difference? Very much so. Consider the punctuation of Hamlet in the Folio, ruminating over his dissociation towards the world, and everything in it, pleasure and pain:

> O God, O God!
> How weary, stale, flat, and unprofitable
> Seems to me all the uses of this world?
> Fie on't? Oh fie, fie [...]
> That it should come to this:
> *(Act I, Scene II)*

The compositor certainly had ! available, using it for Hamlet's exasperated plea to God, but chose ? for the following lines, perhaps prompted by the interrogative 'how', or sensing the prince of Denmark's doubting tone, or indeed following Shakespeare's manuscript lead (although that is less likely).

Today, editors usually replace ? with !, offering readers a much more decisive Hamlet:

> How weary, stale, flat and unprofitable
> Seem to me all the uses of this world!
> Fie on't, ah fie [...] That it should come to this!

Shakespeare's Folio epitomises the trouble we confront when tracing the development of punctuation, and the exclamation mark in particular.

Did the typesetter follow the punctuation of a manuscript? If so, whose manuscript? Shakespeare's or some copyist's? Or did he have to insert punctuation himself? Did he understand exactly the function of each mark, or was he unsure and hoping for the best with each choice? What kind of type did he have available, and did the presence or absence of marks influence his choice?

While the majority of people, including Ralph Crane and his colleagues, struggled with the difference between an exclamation and a question, and played it safe by focusing on 'O' exclamations for the terminal !, some authors insisted on an expansive playing field for enthusiastic clamouring. The prefatory material of the Folio includes poems by Shakespeare's contemporaries, celebrating the 'sweet swan of Avon!', the 'soul of the age!', the 'applause! delight! the wonder of our stage!'. Those exclamations embody Alpoleio's original intention for the exclamation mark: an irrepressible declaration of wonder. And they are,

EXCLAMA'TION. *n.f.* [*exclamatio*, Latin.]
1. Vehement outcry; clamour; outrageous vociferation.
   The ears of the people are continually beaten with *exclama-tions* againſt abuſes in the church. *Hooker, Dedication.*
   Either be patient, and intreat me fair,
   Or with the clamorous report of war
   Thus will I drown your *exclamations. Shakeſp. Richard* III.
2. An emphatical utterance; a pathetical ſentence.
   O' Muſidorus! Muſidorus! but what ſerve *exclamations,*
   where there are no ears to receive the ſound? *Sidney, b.* ii.
3. A note by which a pathetical ſentence is marked thus !

Dr Johnson lays down the law in his 1765 *Dictionary*.

of course, Ben Jonson's. Jonson being Jonson, we can trust his prickly over-involvement in the correct reflection of his poetic contribution to the Folio, from spelling to punctuation.

In the course of the seventeenth century, punctuation as a whole settled into the system we are familiar with today, and the question and exclamation marks grew distinct. The first record of ! as 'note of exclamation' is from a 1656 guide to rhetoric, and indeed the field of influence of ! enlarged, encompassing any eruption of passion or 'pathetical sentence' as Dr Johnson writes in his *Dictionary* of 1765. ! has finally made its mark.

— !!! —

Exclamation marks seemed a perfect fit for the age of sensibility, which puts a premium on refined feelings in men and women. Perhaps as a reaction to the perceived cool rationality of the early eighteenth-century Enlightenment, sensibility celebrated emotions, making the occasional ! more permissible than before. Sensibility, however, when carried to the extreme, could morph into an overly mannered culture of delicate affectation, sparking a new competing trend that celebrated genuine spontaneous emotion, perceived as natural, and thus holy, and its agent was !.

In his *Essay on Punctuation* of 1785, Joseph Robertson calls the exclamation mark 'the voice of nature, when she is agitated, amazed, or transported', particularly 'seemly' for poetry where ! can append 'any kind of emotion', or even just imitate a loud voice (for example, Robertson suggests, Shakespeare's King Richard III's call for 'A horse, a horse! A kingdom for a horse!').

If ! is permissible for poetry, it's less so for prose: Robertson warns the 'young and inexperienced writer against immoderate use' of the exclamation mark which, when over-populating the pages, hints at a text 'full of unnatural reveries, rant, and bombast'. Shockingly, Robertson notes, there are even some 'fanatics' who would smuggle ! into the Bible, twisting its 'sober majesty' into undignified screeching. An avalanche of !!!s as a sign of an unhinged mind? That stigma would stick. Today, we still suspect (surely unfairly) that someone who uses one ! too many teeters on the outer limit of reason. That such blame arose at all, however, was proof that after a century of confusion the workings of ! were well understood at last. It also witnesses the full membership of punctuation to the canon of writing – in fact, perhaps a little too much.

— !!! —

The eighteenth century saw a boom in publications on uniform spelling, grammar and style, and punctuation was not spared: book after book would offer countless rules and examples – only to escape into 'anything goes', according to the taste of the writer. After an exhaustive overview of current punctuation custom, David Steele, in his *Elements of Punctuation* (1786), concludes that punctuation marks 'may be so variably felt, by different people, that two will seldom agree'. If in doubt, add a mark.

During the nineteenth century, the exclamation mark became less and less common. Or should that be exclamation point? A generation or two after America split itself from the British Empire, we also see a shift in punctuation terms: while both the US and UK originally referred to the sign as the 'exclamation point' or 'note', the name now current in Britain and most of its former colonies, 'exclamation mark', completely replaced the old word in the course of the Victorian age.

It is difficult to trace quite when and why this change occurred: it's possible the break happened in the 1860s, when there was an intensely anti-American atmosphere in Britain in consequence of the economic and political wrestling between the two, exacerbated by the American Civil War. Alternatively (or additionally), the modification may have happened in the classrooms: hundreds of teaching grammars circulated at the time, and a consensus for 'mark' could have emerged from there. It's also likely that (for some reason or other) 'interrogation point' became 'question mark' in those early to mid-nineteenth-century decades, and that the exclamation point followed suit.

Mark or point, by the beginning of the twentieth century, Victorian commas, colons and semicolons seemed like the exaggerated trappings of a bygone era: modernity meant a new minimalism. Grammarians and stylists issued warnings against using too many fussy marks and an overly exclamatory tone. One of the most influential guides on English grammar and style of the past hundred or so years, *The King's English* (1906) by Henry and Francis Fowler, did not mince its words: 'what reads wrongly if the stops are

H.W. Fowler, the man who created *The King's English* and set modern exclamatory rules.

removed is radically bad; stops are not to alter meaning, but merely to show it up.' If you need punctuation as a crutch, better not write at all. The Fowlers promote straightforward structures and an uncluttered look. Witty and whimsical, the guide has the authors' personalities written all over it: 'a certain gathering of commas [...] is a suspicious circumstance' and 'anyone who finds himself putting down several commas close to one another should reflect that he is making himself disagreeable'.

The Fowlers' attitude towards language, and their distrust of ! in particular, still have an influence today. Their rules on exclamations are much like the rules of the Ministry of Education a hundred years later in 2016. The exclamation mark is acceptable for sentences starting with 'how' or 'what', for example (as in 'What a difference it makes!'), and for interjections like 'Hell!' and 'oh!'. Unlike eighteenth-century stylists, however, the Fowlers rated some exclamations as more exclamatory than others: 'You surprise me, How dare you?, Don't tell such lies, are mere statement, question, & command, not converted into exclamations by the fact that those who say them are excited, nor to be decorated into You surprise me!, How dare you!, Don't tell such lies!'. In other words, ! is decoration only. It prettifies your sentence, but it's not essential. It doesn't carry gravity.

Similar to all grammarians before them, however, the Fowlers silently embraced defeat by eventually offering confusing, contradictory and idiosyncratic examples: 'He learnt at last that the enemy was – himself!' is correct; 'that is a lie!' is not. They leave us with a stern admonition that 'excessive use of exclamation marks is [...] one of the things that betray the uneducated'.

— !!! —

While the Fowlers were trying to prune the (to them) messy growth of punctuation, elsewhere in the world languages were importing those very signs that the English linguists were hoping to get rid of. In the 1890s and early 1900s, Arab intellectuals feared that the ongoing intrusion of French and English into life in Egypt, Morocco and other culturally and politically colonised countries would lead to an erosion of Arabic as viable language of written expression. Up to that point, reading and writing in Arabic required long years of training, particularly since only few marks such as stylised decorative flowers were used to separate sentences and clarify meaning. Anybody who was not a theologian or other kind of academic would write in French or English, which atrophied the vitality and relevance of Arabic. Lebanese woman writer Zaynab Fawwaz

Zaynab Fawwaz, the introducer of punctuation into Arabic.

was the first to advocate the importation of European punctuation into Arabic in 1893 and, while there were some punctuation experiments to find Arabic's own signs, the literati of the day eventually settled for Western marks with the same functions and shapes, only mirrored from right to left. !, being a symmetrical form, though, exclaims in the same way, be it Swedish or Arabic.

Apart from political choices, new technological advances in the production and circulation of words also ushered in change. A revolutionary moment occurred in the USA in 1867, when the first portable typewriter became available.

Invented by Christopher Latham Shole and sold to the now famous Remington Arms Company, the typewriter was first and foremost intended for business use, and contained the alphabet, numbers, a dollar sign (of course), and a dot and dash – but no !. The omission becomes understandable if one takes into account the machine's initial commercial habitat, which had little need for exclaiming. And, if there ever were such a need, typists would punch a full stop, backspace and superimpose an apostrophe above the dot, just as the mark's inventor and Shakespearean printers did. In fact, a dedicated ! typewriter key continued to be so rare that the 1973 *Secretary's Manual* still explained how to create one by performing the dot-apostrophe manoeuvre.

If it's cumbersome to generate an exclamation mark, users will think twice about it, before they break their flow to perform some back-and-forth gymnastics with the mechanical carriage, lever and keys of the typewriter. It's possible that the exclamation mark's absence on the Remington spilled over into broader attitudes towards language and its functional purpose distilled into the kind of grammar guidance by the Fowler brothers.

The typewriter changed the world of work, making business communication more reliable and faster. The telegraph, developed just a generation before, turned communication upside down, increasing both the speed and the geographical reach of information exchange. While news did travel faster, it needed to be condensed into a nugget, or bytesized, as we'd say today. No space for pesky emotions and even peskier punctuation, as language was flattened out to keep a story intelligible.

However, it was two journalist-novelists whose supposedly neutral style represented the apotheosis of stripped-down expression, and hugely influenced attitudes to emphatic punctuation. One will be hard-pressed to find many !s in the works of Ernest Hemingway and Albert Camus, for whom all blatant expressions of feeling were anathema. A mother's death or the horrors of war are told in a sober tone of apparent objectivity, a full-stop-heavy style, deliberately withholding exclamation marks, perhaps in an attempt to shock the reader into emotion all the more, perhaps to shield from the gravity ! can evoke. Perhaps both.

Yet the punching power of ! would become a potent tool not for irreverent art but for propaganda and publicity in the decades after the free and flirtatious Roaring Twenties. A well-placed ! provided an extra burst of oomph in Second World War propaganda posters on all sides,

Exclamation marks abound in this Colgate advertisement from 1939, with its suggestive text ('*penetrating* foam gets into hidden crevices') for the young woman intent on marriage.

inspiring enthusiasm and endurance in the population at large, especially those whose wartime effort was located in unfamiliar activities like working outside the home. ! as agent of manipulation was useful after the war, too: an easy way of addressing consumers in a friendly and approachable manner was to slap an exclamation mark at the end of the line, particularly in direct speech. It was a device not lost on advertising copywriters.

But !'s true modern home was yet to come: the ease with which our smartphone keypads can produce ! with one click, as well as the instant informality and imitation of real-time speech of social media platforms like Facebook, Twitter and WhatsApp have opened the floodgates for an exploding exclamation mark use for all and any kinds of exclamations. !, !!, !!!, !!!!!!!!!!!!!!!!!!!!!!!! – just when exactly is it one ! too many?

From medieval parchment to modern hypertext, from dotted apostrophes to one-click wonders – the invention, survival and recent thriving of the exclamation mark attests to the crucial task it fulfils in written communication: capturing the spontaneity of a sudden burst of voice. 'Pathetical' the exclamation mark may be, seeing how concerned it is with the passions or feelings. But certainly not pathetic!

CHAPTER TWO

The period that blew its top
Thinking and feeling!

Colons and semicolons are blue; commas and quotation marks green; and full stops, question marks, and exclamation marks red. Or so data visualisation specialist Adam Calhoun proposed in his 2016 designs, representing the punctuational patterns of literary masterpieces by Charles Dickens, James Joyce and Cormac McCarthy.

Dickens preferred long continuous sentences, showing up as all cool blue. Joyce's *Ulysses* is a mixture of colours, as one would expect from a book that experiments with genres, styles and points of view. McCarthy's *Blood Meridian* fires up hot red all over, which makes sense considering his distaste for punctuation: 'I believe in periods, in capitals, in the occasional comma, and that's it,' he told Oprah Winfrey in a rare interview in 2008, saying all other 'weird little marks' do nothing but 'block the page'. McCarthy contends 'if you write properly you

shouldn't have to punctuate.' Clearly a disciple of the
Fowler brothers' school of language. 'You're not all
comma-ed up!' Oprah comments laughingly, suggesting
that the comma clogs the page like some kind of verbal
constipation.

There's a lot to consider in examining the differences
in punctuation between these three authors: the narrowing
of the punctuation range over each sixty-year period
presented in the heatmap examples; the input of editors;
the different narrative voices employed; the subjects and
themes; the length of sentences; and of course individual
authorial tastes. Dickens's long sentences – including

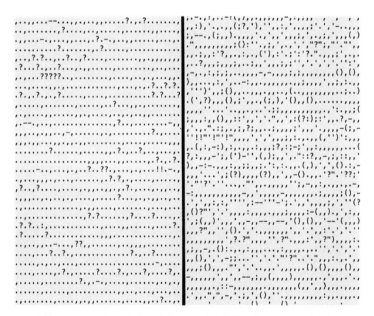

A literary map from Adam Calhoun, visualising the punctuation in
Cormac McCarthy's *Blood Meridian* (left) alongside William
Faulkner's exclamatorily titled *Absalom, Absalom!*.

pages-long descriptions of London fog, for example –
need more punctuation marks than McCarthy's cinemato-
graphic snapshots of the American West. His chunky
sentences ask for less orchestration than, say, the monster-
sentences of a William Faulkner, spreading over hundreds
of words (his longest weighs in at 1,600 words).

Punctuation is a minefield of choice and chance, so
Calhoun's maps will only tell us so much about these
books. Perhaps they're more of an artistic stunt from a
data visualiser, but they make provocative assumptions
about the relationship between grammar and punctuation
by grouping together certain marks, to the exclusion of
others: some (such as ; and :) continue the sentence,
others end it. Exclamation marks, Calhoun claims, have
the same grammatical function as a full stop, emphasising
their syntactical role over their power to capture and
evoke feeling.

This is a radical reclaiming of the role of ! as sentence
terminator with grammatical power over its 'mere' emotion
articulation. ! doesn't just do feeling: it also does serious
syntax. People in the past knew this: the Renaissance
writer John Hart declared that the 'interrogative or admirative' sentences are the 'most full sentences of themselves,
& therefore are also marked with the full sentence point or
prick in the line, adding thereto' the curve and the vertical
slash of ? and !. Like the full stop, question and exclamation marks slam the syntactic brakes, when a unit of
thought is over. But it's not only that they partake of the
period's grammatical lordship over the tempo of words:
they do the double job of negotiating both structure and

tone. Creative writing trainer Noah Lukeman describes ! as 'the period that blew its top', acknowledging its grammatical operation, while suggesting its choleric explosion into visible passion.

One doesn't even have to go as far as Lukeman, and impute irascibility (or other such inconvenient phenomena as feelings). The twins ! and ? indicate the tone of a phrase, and that's both literally (what we need to do with our voice) and metaphorically (the quality of what is being uttered). ? makes us lift our voice (in our heads or throats); ! presses it into emphasis and loudness. ? hints at insecurity and doubt; ! forcefully emits surprise, delight or outrage.

— !!! —

More than the full stop, the exclamation and question mark help comprehend what is being said above and beyond the semantic content of the text. The visionary Hart muses how it would be more 'reasonable to use them before than after, because their tunes do differ from our other manner of pronunciation at the beginning of the sentence'. Sadly, Hart then retracts his judicious proposal, stating 'the matter is of no great moment'.

Clarifying intonation was of sufficient import to the Spanish Royal Academy, however, which lobbied for upside-down versions of ¡ and ¿ at the start of sentences, followed by their closing siblings the right side up at the end. This makes perfect sense, now as it did in 1754. It notifies us of the grammatical and tonal status of the sentence, and helps us match our voice and expectations to it. So, why are we

¡Ay caramba!

Exclamatory bookends make perfect sense in Spanish – and especially so in Bart Simpson's catchphrase (and his first words when he saw his parents having sex).

not universally prefixing questions and exclamations with upside-down marks? Perhaps because existing textual pointers of grammar and word choices are enough to know the immediate direction of a sentence. Possibly because doubling a mark does crowd the page somewhat.

Perhaps also for the same reason that it took more than a hundred years for the Spanish Royal Academy's recommendation to trickle through to day-to-day use: we like ambiguity. We like the uncertainty of not quite knowing what exactly this sentence says. Our brains like decoding equivocal things, be they fuzzy forms or mixed messages. An object emerging from the swirl of shapes and colours in a painting by Miró, or the gentle tugging into this and that direction in the gently teasing dialogue of a Jane Austen novel. Perfect sense ready-made doesn't interest us. We like being challenged by that which we don't understand.

The reasons for tone-fixing schemes, particularly by authorities like the Royal Academy's, are clear: ambiguity (though we feel drawn to it) makes us nervous. Irony does, too. Saying one thing, and meaning another, but what? Writers and thinkers across centuries have both revelled in language's contradictory carnival of meaning, and attempted to nail down its elusiveness again and again through ever more elaborate new punctuation marks. Irony and its harsher cousin sarcasm (irony with a bite) have particularly exercised the imagination of punctuation proposers, and continue to do so in our digital age. Some of those new punctuation ideas are gimmicky brainchildren, never intended to join the lofty regions of grammar where comma and full stop reign supreme; others are serious schemes from earnest experimenters of language, trying to improve communication with their contribution of a new sign to convey a particular thought or a feeling. The latter are attempting to capture and control unruly meaning; the former experiments are highlighting the absurdity of any such endeavour.

In spite of all our attempts, language keeps slipping through the net, refusing to be caught. This elusiveness both puzzles and fascinates us: we love the challenge of chasing for sense; and we also hunger for neat explanations. Punctuation is a site of contention where we can see those two contradictory needs jostle for prominence, never winning out.

— ! ! ! —

 The quest to clarify the meaning of words that are disembodied from vocal inflections or body language began during the Renaissance: in 1575, English printer Henry Denham included a mirrored question mark for 'percontations', questions that don't have a yes or no

Thomas Middleton, *A Game at Chess* manuscript (1624), Act II, Scene I. Note the two percontation points: 'hows to mes'.

answer, but accommodate manifold answers, including those that require none. The percontation point thus marked rhetorical questions, its name coming from the Latin for 'through' (*per*) and 'spear' (*contus*): a rhetorical question is so penetrating that it pierces like a lance. Perhaps Denham was prompted by the authors whose work he printed, and who might have demanded some such sign, or perhaps he invented the percontation point for himself. Denham was certainly curious about new trends in literature and text production, importing the semicolon from Italy a little later, in the 1580s. The reverse question mark did not catch on, although it kicks around in seventeenth-century manuscripts, for example by the poet and priest Robert Herrick, and Shakespeare's contemporary and fellow-playwright Thomas Middleton.

Around a hundred years after Denham, another Englishman cast around for a way to flag up irony. Just like his predecessor, John Wilkins played around with the directionality of existing marks, and turned the question mark not from right to left, but upside down. Wilkins was searching for ways to edit error out of language in order to reduce miscommunication, one of the primary reasons for human misery, he felt. A scientist and co-founder of the Royal Society, he proposed a universal language made from symbols which represented concepts rather than words or sounds. Wilkins hoped to repair what he saw as the faultiness of the languages of the world: diversity and, emerging from that, diversity of opinion. That's why Wilkins (meticulous scientist as he was) worried over the details of expression, convinced that small things matter. Punctuation matters. Trying to control language, however, is always misguided, and sometimes doomed, and so, because the interesting things happen in those gaps, Denham's ꜱ and Wilkins' ¿ sunk into oblivion. But not the desire to imprison ambiguity.

In 1708, author and military strategist Jean-Léonor Le Gallois de Grimarest demanded a whole host of new punctuation marks to assist readers in getting the tone of the writer, including a point of commandment, mistrust point, anger point, love point, hate point, joy point, pain point and irony point. He was probably serious about it, unlike

— Philos. *Ironie socratique* V. la partie encycl.
— Typogr. *Point d'ironie,* Signe particulier, proposé par Alcanter de Brahm, pour indiquer au lecteur les passages, les phrases ironiques d'un ouvrage, d'un article.
— Encycl. Littér. *L'ironie* est, en rhétorique, ou un trope ou une figure de pensée. Elle consiste, dans l'un et l'autre cas, à dire le contraire de ce qu'on pense, de telle manière que le lecteur ou l'auditeur comprenne le sens caché sous cette raillerie. « Bon apôtre ! », « L'homme de bien ! », en parlant d'un fripon, voilà la figure de mots. La figure de pensée commence dès que l'ironie se développe en une suite de propositions ou de phrases. Tel livre de *Gargantua,* tel passage de la satire *Ménippée,* telle lettre de Voltaire, les

Point d'ironie.

Alcanter de Brahm makes a case for ironic punctuation.

satirical journalist Marcelin Jobard many years later, who needed more emotion signs to replace 'a mass of little parasitical phrases' (like 'he said mockingly') that 'don't do anything but make discourse longer and heavier'. In his 1839 *Lacunes de la Typographie*, he proposed a multi-purpose spade-like shape whose arrow, pointing in different direction, indicates irritation, indignation, hesitation – and irony (adding, tongue-in-cheek, that its purpose was to 'avoid duels').

At the end of the century, French humorist Alcanter de Brahm revamped the percontation point to signify irony, with moderate success: the *Nouveau Larousse Illustré* of 1897–1905 contains the mark under the heading 'irony'.

― !!! ―

If the shape of the question mark, however distorted, has dominated experimentation with irony points for centuries, the twentieth century brought ! back into the fray to approximate that most elusive of tones. Alcanter de Brahm's *point d'ironie* has an exclamation body and a questioning head, capturing the mixture of wonder, surprise, outrage and astonishment that can accompany irony, or rhetorical questions. The Cambridge scholar I.A. Richards proposes a set of 'special symbols' in his 1942 volume *How to Read a Page*. In the same vein as Marcellin Jobard a century before him, but seriously, he advocates a reduction of textual traffic by deploying symbols that would 'abridge both the visual and intellectual labour of the reader' by hugging certain words like hovering footnote numbers, signalling the tone or function in the sentence. He suggests a doubled 'nb' (for 'nota bene') to mark turning-point words, and a twinned 'q' for 'query' (as in 'the meaning of this word needs to be explored'). He also has paired exclamation marks, as in this example, in which he mocks another literary critic, admonishing: 'Do not let us mistake the grounds for such mistrust of psychology with the !evidence! he fished up against it.'

Are we to shriek out the exclamation-marked word when reading aloud, or with a voice in our heads? Or is seeing derision enough to deride? It's not altogether clear what Richards wants us to do, either with the raised exclamations or with the rest of his innovations (little wonder they never caught on), but his choice of the exclamation

   ❝......❝   indicates that our problem is, What does this word say here? Not whether anything it seems to say is acceptable or not. The marks are equivalent to Query: what meaning? There is no derogatory implication. Most ᵠimportantᵃ passages are, or should be, in this situation.

   ¹......¹   indicates surprise or derision, a Good Heavens! What-a-way-to-talk! attitude. It should be read ¹shriek¹ if we have occasion to read it aloud.

   ⁿᵇ......ⁿᵇ   indicates that how the word is understood is a turning point in the discussion, and usually that it may easily be read in more than one way or with an inadequate perception of its importance. The sign is short for *Nota Bene.*

A trio from I.A. Richards' proposals for a set of special symbols in his 1942 book, *How to Read a Page.*

mark for a mocking effect shows that the time of ! as a baseline for alternative marks had come.

Twenty years after Richards, French writer Hervé Bazin published a teasing manifesto for language reforms that also contained proposals on new 'intonation points': the love point (two apprehensive question marks, tenderly leaning towards one another while rooted in the same dot, forming a provisional heart), the conviction mark (shaped

like a cross), the authority point ('like a sultan's parasol', Bazin writes), the irony point in the form of a ! with extended arms (or the Greek letter Ψ – psi – a contemptuous sound we make when scoffing at someone), the acclamation point (like the victory sign, 'arms lifted' in triumph), and, finally, the point of doubt – jagged, torn apart by hesitation as to which side to fall.

— !!! —

In the second half of the twentieth century, there followed several new punctuation marks which never made it beyond the pages they featured in, such as the indignation point by Raymond Queneau, and the very necessary 'point of shit' by disruptive French poet Michel Ohl, to be used, for example, in addressing your local incapable politician. The

ω exclamation mark here provides the core structure around which typographic playfulness unfurls, with the two cheeks of a punctuation bottom squeezing out a **!** of ink.

We still want to nail down irony in our digital age, but we've given up on punctuation-like symbols altogether: ironics, or *backwards-slanting italics*, for sarcastic remarks, arrived in 1990s chatrooms; in 2001, blogger pioneer Tara Liloia proposed a tilde after the undermined word (you're so smart ~); and in 2010 came the one-eyed snail trademarked as SarcMark (available for $1.99 only!!! ℒ). The SarcMark inventors received an undue amount of flak for their suggestion – presumably because they are the only experimenters seeking to monetise their punctuation play. Then along came Twitter and, with it, meta-comment on one's own comment #sarcasm. That practice morphed into its written form ('hashtag sarcasm'), which itself seeped into colloquial speech. In the past couple of years, we've abandoned words altogether and clung to pictures a little too desperately, perhaps. Will the emoji save us from the perils of faceless communication?

The closest to a successful new mark to inscribe tone is perhaps Martin Speckter's 1962 invention, a simple superimposition of **?** and **!**. An advertising agent, Speckter was looking for a mark with which to convey disbelief, indignation, fear and emergency, some thing that 'fits the times [...] when there's a new crisis or calamity almost every day'. Speckter ran a survey in a typography magazine, asking for names for his punctuation concoction. 'Exclamaquest', 'QuizDing' and 'exclarotive' did not make it, but 'interrobang' did, being a fusion of 'interrogation' and 'bang' (a printers term for !). ‽ is not really a new mark at all, but rather two old ones squeezed together. Perhaps that's why it's still only lurking around the edges of typography and text reproduction without full acceptance into the gamut of marks. The 1968 Remington Rand typewriter included its very own interrobang key, and a few years later you were able to buy an extra key to manually screw onto your Smith Corona typewriter, so there must have been some interest in and understanding of the new sign – but not enough to keep it alive. The interrobang fled into a passive existence in Unicode, the system of unique numbers for every character in every language, workable on every device or coding program. ‽ lingers on in a few select typefaces (among them the playful Calibri ‽).

The interrobang's birth is not dissimilar to the invention of the semicolon in 1492 by the Venetian master printer Aldo Manuzio. The Italian merged the comma and the colon to signify a nuanced pause between the shorter and the

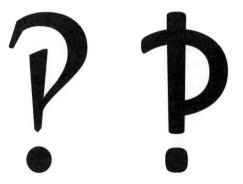

Two variations of the interrobang – Palatino (left) and Calibri.

longer rest, both of breath and of thought. A most subtle distinction. Although one of the rarities of punctuation, the semicolon is still with us today, perhaps because it precisely does not deal in tone, but pause. Tonal punctuation experiments seem doomed to fail. Like its predecessors, the interrobang has quietly died the death that most new marks do. Punctuation history is littered with such casualties: what we don't need, we don't keep. Who would want to decode the deliciously mysterious pleasures of irony, anyway‽ Or should that be 'anyway?!' or 'anyway!?', rather?

— !!! —

One honourable mention of the appearance of ‽ must be made, however, and that's as title of the 1969 thriller *Interrabang*: the film is an Italian *giallo*, a name that comes from cheap mystery novels clad in yellow (*giallo*) paper. *Interrabang* features three beautiful women on an island in the hot Mediterranean, visited on their yacht by a handsome man whose criminal record they don't care much about, even when they find a dead body lying at the bottom of a bay of the island. It's a slow film with lots of attractive tanned bodies, Bardot-esque towers of hair and the suggestion of sex at every steamy moment. The *giallo* is an over-the-top genre, and *Interrabang* is a perfect example. The inter-robang which one of the women is wearing as a huge golden pendant is a fitting symbol for the genre (who murders who? why?), and for the film's shocking finale. Who is the real killer after all? We're still unsure after plenty of plot twists and red herrings. Before the credits, the interrobang looms mockingly on the screen, teasing us with its proudly declarative uncertainty.

— !!! —

Martin Speckter thought the interrobang was not only a suitable sign for emotional expression, but also a symbol of his times, a period of rapid change, of cultural and political upheaval. While the **?** of **‽** stands for our bafflement, **!** proclaims distress. It's the 'bang' of 'interrobang' after all. It packs a punch, and jolts us out of any potential compla-cency. **!** is less about what exactly we exclaim but about the intention motivating the exclamation in the first place: **!** embodies the voice of the author, and it encourages us to take up that voice too. In fact, it not only encourages, but forces us whether we like it or not. We become whatever the writer was when going for **!**. We need **!** to feel. At the same time, we worry about the agency it has over us.

— !!! —

The power of the exclamation mark to orchestrate tone and feeling makes us nervous, at least some of us. **!** has a foot in both camps: grammar and rhetoric; cold hard rule and fuzzy emotion. It sits perched between syntactical exactness and blurry subjectivity, revelling in its double identity, a queer mark that defies binaries if ever there was one.

It's precisely this queerness, which can't be boxed into square categories, that has some language sticklers up in arms. Such refusal to be one or the other is too excessive, and so is its power over our emotions, and its often doubled, tripled and quadrupled appearance in a conga line of !!!!s. Vitriol against exclamation marks abounds in grammars and style guides, warning against their use in anything but personal communication, and even in that over-use is a 'sign of undisciplined writing', as *The Blue Book of Grammar* advises: 'do not use even one of these marks unless you're convinced it is justified'. *The Penguin Guide to Punctuation* asserts that ! can come across as 'breathless, almost childish', and the almighty *Chicago Manual of Style* allocates not even a single full page to exclamation mark use, restricting it to outcries and ironic or emphatic comments.

This is not surprising, considering the scepticism *The Chicago Manual* shows towards the wayward potential of dots and dashes: the purpose of punctuation 'is to promote the ease of reading by clarifying relationships within and between sentences'. Although *The Chicago Manual* graciously allows some leeway, punctuation 'should in turn be governed by the consistent application of some basic principles lest the subjective element obscure meaning'. This is paying mere lip service to flexibility, fundamentally mistrusting the liveliness of language. Grammars, guides, governments – all of those who prescribe how to speak and write, and who punish whenever there is deviance from what they deem correct, are worried about the uncontrollable abundance of language, its proclivity for excess and lawlessness, its subversion of neat categories. ! infuses messiness (aka life) into orderly disembodied glyphs on pristine white paper. ! is at the service of language's joyful jungle. The rules are not timeless, or universal. Punctuation is neither a God-given system, nor a natural element of language, but a 'set of practices of varying rigour' as linguist David Crystal puts it.

It's vague and nebulous, depending on who writes what for whom with which technology at what time. The !!!-filled text to your best friend is going to allow for different grammar and punctuation than a hand-signed letter to your lawyer. Punctuation that's effective for the textual situation varies accordingly. Yet the self-styled grammar police, as much as publishers, teachers and official institutions, feels entitled to measure, assess and punish our writing.

— !!! —

This stifling attitude towards language, and punctuation in particular, has not always been prevalent. In fact, it's only in the past two hundred years or so that we've become addicted to rules (or what we perceive as such). The first English grammar guide was the 1586 *Pamphlet for Grammar* by William Bullokar. Between then and 1700, some 16 further grammars of English were printed, a number that rose past 270 in the eighteenth century – which was nothing compared to the nineteenth-century explosion of 900 volumes of rules and regulations. Grammars were a true publishing phenomenon on both sides of the Atlantic.

The rapid evolution of the book-manufacturing and bookselling businesses certainly contributed to this increased output, as did the rising level of literacy among a range of social groups, groups who may have sought upward progress through 'correct' and 'proper' language. But, as we saw in the previous chapter, a gentleman cares not at all about dotting his i's and crossing his t's. Technology, education and social mobility are not the whole story for the paper tsunami of grammars: the surge in linguistic consciousness during the eighteenth century goes hand in hand with developments in the natural sciences. Grammarians attempted to align the analysis of language with those developments, putting a premium on the categorisation of unchangeable relationships and rules.

If language was a science, there must be a definitive way of constructing and punctuating sentences. In their quest to define language as a stable system with comprehensive laws and specific methods analogous to, say, optics or mathematics, grammarians not only described the conventions that writers were adhering to at the time, but also injected some rules of their own into the bewildering proliferation of decrees – sometimes as a last resort to fill the number of pages promised to the publisher! Among those contributing to the growth of grammar regulations was Bishop Lowth, who chose to

> So that the doctrine of Punctuation must needs be very imperfect: few precise rules can be given, which will hold without exception in all cases; but much must be left to the judgement and taste of the writer.

Bishop Lowth's grammar: leaving some room for doubt.

stigmatise the split infinitive, the double negative and the placement of a preposition at the end of a sentence. His hugely influential *A Short Introduction to English Grammar* (1762) was reprinted annually for the next forty years, sometimes more often than once a year, and even served as a basic grammar book for some schools until the beginning of the twentieth century.

Although Lowth has a reputation as founder of grammatical dogmatism, it is unfair to cast him as a killer of creativity. He admits: 'few precise rules can be given, which will hold without exception in all cases'. Punctuation is particularly 'imperfect', so that 'much must be left to the judgement and taste of the writer'. Lowth recommends we make do with what we have, arguing we can keep inventing new signs as much as we want, but they would 'perplex us and rather be a hindrance, not an assistance'.

For all these attempts to infer rules of grammar and punctuation with general applicability, eighteenth-century grammarians and stylists actually had a far more relaxed attitude towards language than they are often given credit for. When they offer a rule, they follow it with examples from literature or other kinds of writing, which tend to demonstrate that truly effective style and punctuation is contextual, and cannot in fact be taught, but must be acquired slowly, as if by osmosis. If you want to be a good writer, read good writing.

— !!! —

During the Victorian age, we started to take eighteenth-century prescriptivism too seriously, doing away with examples in favour of the blunt artificial rule. Punctuation was no longer a motley matter of effectiveness, textual genre, context and personal taste – a baggy, imprecise and capacious creature. Instead, it was a delineation of syntax only, without voice, without personality. Without !.

What the grammar police don't know, however, or conveniently don't see, is that grammar is not about rules, and that rules are historical, anyway. They are historical, and as such are subject to change according to the choice of those using the language. Today's rule is no rule tomorrow: a little over a hundred years ago, for instance, separating items on a simple list was within the remit of the semicolons, but few of us would choose them nowadays. Systematisation gives us a sense of security, but it is a false sense. Something is a rule because we collectively buy into it. Grammar doesn't help us to win a prize for correct answers, but rather offers a rough map of how a language behaves, so that we can feel our way into it. Rules are more like ever-developing zones between which language is doing its things, accommodating the conventionally 'right' and the conventionally 'not so right'. Whether certain punctuation works has to be adjudicated on a case-by-case basis. There's no 'one size fits all'.

— !!! —

In the afterword of her 1974 book *Woman Hating*, feminist writer Andrea Dworkin describes how her text had been altered from grammatically devious to blandly

Andrea Dworkin's Argument
Against Punctuation

'my publisher changed my punctuation because book reviewers (Mammon) do not like lower case letters, fuck (in the old sense) book reviewers (Mammon)' – Andrea Dworkin states her case.

normal. Her lower case letters had been raised, her lack of apostrophes redressed, and punctuation added wherever deemed necessary – punctuation which she calls 'garbage'. Punctuation, Dworkin believes, shackles the text and the reader. It imposes order on the disorder in which she invites us to revel. Punctuation (just like dress and sexuality) are part and parcel of oppressive 'standard forms', also known as conventions.

'Conventions are mightier than armies,' she claims, 'police, and prisons. each citizen becomes the enforcer, the doorkeeper, and instrument of the Law, an unfeeling guard punching his fellow men hard in the belly'. Dworkin would laugh at the absurdity of downgrading school children for a 'wrong' exclamation mark. 'Standard forms' means dealing with a text from a distance, wary of the power it can have over our impressionable minds. On the other hand, a text 'violating standard forms means changing one's way of thinking'. It means 'not to think about different things, but to think differently'. ! wants us to do just that.

'so !f!'

Literature and the flaming pink scarf

Whichever grammar guide one consults, punctuation advice on ! is usually short (one page, two at a push), because it seems intuitively clear how to use it. Style guides tend to focus on advising against using the mark at all, rather than on how to use it more. That's where Russian writer Anton Chekhov's satirical genius steps in: in his 1885 short story 'The Exclamation Point', Chekhov stages the torments of a man who is driven to distraction by the problem of !. Minor clerk Perekladin, a copyist of documents, is accused by a young man at a reception of having insufficient education for such a respectable position. Defensive, Perekladin alleges that the copying of 'documents' requires no education. Spelling, punctuation, none of them pose a problem if one 'just puts them in correctly' and out of 'habit'. The young man disagrees, claiming 'it is not enough to put it in correctly' – one needs to include punctuation 'consciously'. Else it's only 'mechanical reproduction'!

This bugs Perekladin so much that he tosses and turns at night, dreaming about punctuation marks, which emerge

Anton Chekhov (left) with Leo Tolstoy, photographed in 1902.

from the dark sky as gleaming shapes, requiring him to state their rules of use before disappearing. Meteoric commas and falling star colons flash and vanish, as the poor dreamer becomes more and more confident in his punctuation skills, until one mark trips him up badly: it's !, and he doesn't know how to use it. Distressed by this, Perekladin shakes his wife awake, and asks about the rules for !, which she (with her boarding school education) easily offers: it's used for 'appeals, exclamations, expressions of delight, indignation, joy, anger, and other feelings'. Feelings ... the clerk ruminates. In forty years of service, and thousands upon thousands of lines of words, he has never had to deal with feelings. 'But is there any need for feelings in documents?' he wonders.

Such an attitude, of course, will be revenged. ! now haunts Perekladin mercilessly, peeping out from behind his wife's shoulder, dancing in candle flames and sticking to the boots of passers-by. 'Machine! Writing machine!' it mocks him. 'Unfeeling block of wood!' The clerk loses his mind over the obsessively appearing sign, rushes to work in a frenzy, and signs the Christmas card for his boss with his name followed by three triumphant !!!s, finally feeling all those hitherto repressed feelings of delight, indignation, joy, and most of all anger. Now exorcised, the 'fiery exclamation mark was satisfied and vanished'.

Where there is humanness, there is !. The polar opposite of a soberly analytical clerk's file, a literary text, is not a free-for-all either, however: if a writer needs a trio of !!!s to make a scene come alive, opinion goes, they had better re-examine said scene. Creative writing adviser Noah

Lukeman characterises ! as 'the bright green dress, the flaming pink scarf', adding there 'may be an occasion, once every five years, when it is needed; until then, like those clothes, it is best left in the closet'. The exclamation mark is just too flashy and attention-grabbing for its own good, too cheap a thrill for Serious Literature. It's good, then, that writers tend not to follow writing advice, least of all their own.

American crime and thriller writer Elmore Leonard is strict on !: 'You're not allowed more than two or three per 100,000 words of prose.' Yet he uses sixteen times the amount of permissible exclamations himself. Data journalist Ben Blatt has crunched the numbers for us, revealing an inverse ratio of number of novels and exclamation marks used in the authors selected for comparison.

The fewer books you write, the greater the number of outbursts, it might seem. This is a debatable conclusion (it presupposes that books are of a uniform length), but Blatt also claims that the more unpractised (or luckless) the writer, the higher the number of exclamation marks:

Elmore Leonard	45 Novels	49
Ernest Hemingway	10 Novels	59
John Updike	26 Novels	88
Michael Chabon	7 Novels	91
Neil Gaiman	7 Novels	96
Chuck Palahniuk	14 Novels	106
William Faulkner	19 Novels	108
Toni Morrison	10 Novels	111

Number of !s per 100,00 words. From Ben Blatt's *Nabokov's Favorite Word is Mauve* (2017).

analysing 9,000 fanfiction pieces, totalling a billion words, published online between 2015 and 2017, Blatt found 392 exclamation marks per 100,000 words on average, more than four times the amount noted in 100 bestsellers and literary award holders of 2017.

Winning Blatt's laurel for the most frequent exclamation marks in a single book is Salman Rushdie's *Midnight's Children* whose total of 2,131 !s make for an average of more than six !s per page. That's a lot of pink scarves. Yet, *Midnight's Children* has also garnered endless accolades, including the Booker Prize of 1981, as well as the Booker of Bookers (twice!), a best-of of all the winners since the prize's inception in 1968.

Clearly, ! can get you noticed.

A worthy contestant for the exclamation crown is bestselling author Tom Wolfe, whose books abound in bold and brash !!!!!!!! fireworks: Wolfe came to public attention with his 1965 miscellany of essays *The Kandy-Kolored Tangerine-Flake Streamline Baby*. Gathering Wolfe's essays for *Esquire* magazine, it takes its title from his essay on kustom kars (pimped rides), originally called 'There goes (VAROOM! VAROOM!) that Kandy Kolored (THPHHHHHH!) tangerine-flake streamline baby (RAHGHHHH!) around the bend (BRUMMMMMMM-MMMMMMMMM......'.

Stretching across the upper third part of two facing pages, the title delights in typographical mischief, scaling up parenthesised sound effects at the expense of the main sentence's content-bearing but fantastical words. The transcriptions of car noises are reminiscent of comic book

Tom Wolfe's *The Kandy-Kolored Tangerine-Flake Streamline Baby*, as originally published in *Esquire* magazine.

speech bubbles, or the language children use in play, and that's perhaps exactly how the owners of kustom kars treat their, well, orange babies. The exclamation marks catapult the bracketed racket out of the page and into our eyes and ears. Note the final expected ! dissolving into the dot dot dot exhaust fumes of the revving kustom kar, speeding out of the magazine.

Wolfe contributed to the development of a new kind of journalism in the 1960s and '70s that introduced the feature story, feeding on fiction elements for non-fiction stories. Moving quickly from scene to scene, Wolfe's journalism is opulent and conversational, even shouty and aggressive. If his journalism borrowed from fiction, his fiction certainly borrowed from his newspaper work: Wolfe's first novel, *Bonfire of the Vanities* (1987), clocks in at approximately 230,000 words, with a whopping 2,400 !s – around three per page. The exclamation mark perfectly suits the book's shrill 1980s vibe, and its exposure of New York as a hotbed mixture of stock-market greed, racial tensions and high-profile court cases. Wolfe masterfully manipulates the urgency ! spreads, jumping at us, and making us jump:

> Harlem rises up! What a show! Not the hustlers and the operators and the players rise up – but Harlem rises up! All of black New York rises up! He's only mayor for some of the people! He's the mayor of White New York! Set fire to the mutt!

Who wouldn't rise, be swept up and away by the power of exclamation?!

— !!! —

Copious fistfuls of !s would become Wolfe's trademark, so much so that his connection to the sign gained cultural currency: at a literature festival celebrating an unlikely poet (Moe Szyslak), Lisa Simpson introduces Wolfe with: 'He uses more exclamation marks than any American author.' To which Wolfe cheerfully replies 'It's true!'. When challenged, the real Wolfe defended his exclamatory style: 'People complain about my exclamation marks, but I honestly think that's the way people think. I don't think people think in essays; it's one exclamation mark to another.' It's curious Wolfe contends we think from ! to !. Perhaps our internal voices are less placid and peaceful than we like to believe.

! can make itself felt through over-presence, but it can also stick out through near-total absence: in *The Old Man and the Sea*, published just before he won the Nobel Prize in 1954, Ernest Hemingway uses a single fateful !, when the old man pulls the fishing line that triggers the events that would be his curse and blessing, depending how one looks at it. Out alone on the sea, the old man realises his streak of bad fishing luck has finally ended, as a creature of gigantic size seems to have taken the bait at last. Waiting for the perfect timing to pull, the old man strategically lets the marling feed:

> Eat it so that the point of the hook goes into your heart and kills you, he thought. Come up easy and let me put the harpoon into you. All right. Are you ready? Have you been long enough at table?
>
> 'Now!' he said aloud and struck hard with both hands, gained a yard of line and then struck again and again, swinging with each arm alternately on the cord with all the strength of his arms and the pivoted weight of his body.

This single exclamation mark – one of just 59 in Hemingway's whole output – has a tremendous job to do, performing that sudden yanking on the line, the excitement of expectation, a change of pace for both the old man and the reader – surely, the monster fish will now go wild at this intrusion into its realm. Surely, 'Now!' rings in the fight of human vs beast. Hemingway, however, continues:

> Nothing happened. The fish just moved away slowly and the old man could not raise him an inch.

A literary anticlimax if ever there was one.

— !!! —

If Blatt were correct in connecting high sales with moderate use of exclamation marks, *Bonfire of the Vanities* and *Midnight's Children* ought not to be as successful as they are, nor should *The Old Man and the Sea* be a bestseller, given its paucity of them. How would we explain those outliers of ! deprivation and ! glut based on Blatt's computerised analysis? Such an analysis of literature lies upon shaky foundations that, more often than not, do not take into account the natural evolution of language and taste: what is a cliché today was not one yesterday, for example. How do we take a writer's stylistic evolution into account when interpreting with statistics? And who says Jane Austen put those !s into *Pride and Prejudice* herself? (Spoiler alert: she didn't.)

The question of whether an author themselves inserted !s in their texts or not is a pertinent one. The presence of a liberal splash of exclamation marks is generally an indication of writerly involvement, since editors are unlikely to introduce something as declarative as !. If Tom Wolfe's reputation rests on a multitude of !s, it's safe to assume he was paying close attention to their survival from manuscript to first edition. The same applies to brave books with ! in their titles, such as *How the Grinch Stole Christmas!* and *Oh, the Places You'll Go!* and *Horton Hears a Who!*

A quarter of Dr Seuss's titles end on the enthusiastic wonderer, but it's not just children's authors who know about the power of the bang: adults love a well-placed

exclamation, too, witness P.G. Wodehouse's *Carry on, Jeeves!* or Jonathan Coe's *What a Carve Up!*, or *Absalom, Absalom!* by Nobel Prize winner William Faulkner. Set before, during and after the American Civil War, Faulkner's novel is loosely inspired by the biblical story of a rebellious child and heartbroken father, whose cry for his son startles the eye as it scans the title page.

Some writers seek to wield maximum control over their works from full stop to finished book. Mark Twain was such an author. For his *Connecticut Yankee at King Arthur's Court*, he ordered the typesetter to 'have no opinion whatever regarding the punctuation, that he was simply to make himself into a machine and follow the copy' – in fact, to become a Perekladin. And we know how well that turns out. Because Twain's typesetters had plenty of feelings and opinions about his commas and colons, the author found himself involved in a battle: when a proof-reader informed him that he was 'improving' his punctuation, Twain responded with 'telegraphed orders to have him shot without giving him time to pray'. A decade later, Twain was still demanding that his publishers should 'restore' his original punctuation, and get rid of their 'insanities', so that he could read the 'purified pages' one last time before being committed to the final printing.

Other writers are distinctly less interested in punctuation, and some are thankful for professional support. At the beginning of his poetic career, Lord Byron asked his publisher John Murray for help: 'Do you know any body who can *stop* – I mean *point* – *commas* and so forth? for I am, I fear, a sad hand at your punctuation.' William Wordsworth felt his poems were safe in the pointing hands of the natural scientist Humphrey Davy, calling himself 'no adept' at the 'business' of punctuation.

— !!! —

But scrutinising a writer's exclamation mark habits is not as straightforward as it seems. Jane Austen, celebrated for her balanced semicolon-patterned style, comes to us through the filter of her original typesetter and editor (and all the subsequent ones). The few remaining manuscripts, however, show a writer who peppers her pages with dashes and exclamation marks, crosses out false starts, adds sentences between lines and blotches her papers as she moves from thought to thought – rather like Tom Wolfe, but in Austen's case we have edited out the breathless punctuation and spontaneousness, perhaps because such an impression of her doesn't fit stereotypical notions of a prim and poised lady author.

So, was Jane Austen in need of several men to massage her slapdash drafts into her now-revered signature style?

Yes and no.

We have a frustratingly small amount of Austen's hand-written material, and almost no manuscripts of her printed work. What we do have, however, are cleaned-up copies of her unpublished first novel, *Lady Susan*, and of early experiments with mini-plays written by the eleven-year-old Jane for her household, which are full of witty mocking observations about the manners of her day, as we might expect of the sharp-eyed satirist she would become. There are also drafts of two unfinished novels (*The Watsons* and *Sanditon*) and two work-in-progress chapters of *Persuasion*, published in 1818, one year after Austen's premature death at the age of 42. This handwritten legacy enlarges the span of Jane's writing career beyond the window of the big six novels, and allows us to chart her authorial development. The *Persuasion* chapters are particularly interesting, since they are the closest we get to what she may have submitted to her publisher: other than those few sheets, we have no proof of how much involve-ment she may or may not have had in the transition from manuscripts to published books.

How do her drafts look in the wild? Take this example from the end of *Persuasion*, in which the heroine Anne and

Captain Wentworth exchange perspectives on their bumpy road to engagement. The original print version reads thus:

'You should have distinguished,' replied Anne. 'You should not have suspected me now; the case so different, and my age so different. If I was wrong in yielding to persuasion once, remember that it was to persuasion exerted on the side of safety, not of risk. When I yielded, I thought it was to duty; but no duty could be called in aid here. In marrying a man indifferent to me, all risk would have been incurred, and all duty violated.'

'Perhaps I ought to have reasoned thus,' he replied, 'but I could not.'

Compare this to the manuscript version, replete with dashes, emphatic underlining and capitalised words:

'You should have distinguished – replied Anne – You should not have suspected me now; – The case so different, & my age so different! – If I was wrong, in yeilding to Persuasion once, remember that it was to Persuasion exerted on the side of Safety, not of Risk. When I yeilded, I thought it was to Duty. – But no Duty could be called in aid here. – In marrying a Man indifferent to me, all Risk would have been incurred, & all Duty violated.'
– 'Perhaps I ought to have reasoned thus, he replied, but I could not. – "

In Austen's handwritten original, her punctuation follows the rhythms of spoken words and intense emotionally

The exclamation mark (eventually edited out) is at the end of the tenth line in this original manuscript of *Persuasion*.

charged turns of phrase. As a teenager, she had written short plays that were performed by her household; as an adult, she kept that ear for dialogue in her prose. Austen's contemporary and fellow writer Samuel Taylor Coleridge believed that punctuation marks are not 'logical symbols but rather dramatic directions representing the process of thinking and speaking'. As such they enable 'the reader more easily to place himself in the state of the writer or original speaker'. They help us feel and think what the character is feeling and thinking. What would Coleridge have said had he known how Austen's punctuation was toned down?

In contrast to the hurried and expressive original, the printed end-product is a smoothed-out thing, lacking the dashes, capitals and erasures that make for an uneven but exciting visual reading experience. Warm and argumentative underlinings and the self-confident ! are gone, leaving a drier, more controlled tone that seems somewhat unlikely for two people who have waited nearly a decade for one another. Rhetorical liveliness has fallen victim to the grammatical axe; true messy feeling, to sober politeness. But the situation is more complicated than that.

Austen expert Professor Kathryn Sutherland postulates that the two chapters are excerpts from a nearly finished version which Austen sent to her publisher John Murray, and that it was poet and literary critic William Gifford who edited *Persuasion* for printing, and probably other of her works, too. Three years before, Murray had already consulted Gifford over whether to add Austen to his list of authors, and he had approved of the already published *Pride and Prejudice* ("'tis very good', only that it is 'so pointed as to be unintelligible').

Gifford read *Emma* in manuscript, and promised to 'readily correct the proof', hoping he 'may do it a little good here & there'. It seems Gifford was concerned mostly with punctuation, and clearly he intended to serve the text, rather than make his mark on it. Since there is not a single page of evidence of Austen correcting printed proofs, or even the manuscripts she definitely did send to the publisher, we cannot know her involvement in the different stages a text went through in its transformation from loose-leafed chrysalis to bound-book butterfly. Did she begrudgingly accept editorial emendation? Or did she expect and perhaps even welcome it as an honour done to her work?

Sutherland calls the passage from manuscript to book the 'socialisation processes of print', because it's a collective effort: it takes a village to make a book; a book needs a whole society of fans cheering it on every step of the way from editor and typesetter to proof-corrector and publisher. But this dispersal of literary agency and control over the text also means making it socially acceptable, taming its dashing exclamatory wildness.

This 'interfering' with the author's now-prized original words and features is really not their problem at all: we today make it our problem, because we seek to get at the 'real' Austen, untrammelled by male meddlers. Is it OK if the grande dame owes her gracefully restrained style to lesser, perhaps even mechanical, hands? Does a female author need our saving from evil editors? Perhaps yes, and perhaps not. It's crucial to be able to access the manuscripts (now digitised) for comparison with the printed versions, and to hold up as a truth yet universally unacknowledged that even the most accomplished writer, in possession of a good manuscript, must be in want of an editor.

Perhaps, rather than to judge a book by the numbers an algorithm spits out about it, we might want to consider what it actually sets out to do, and if it does that well. Ben Blatt's graphs have little to say about that purpose and its punctuation, or Austen's amalgamated co-created mongrel works. Those aspects are unmeasurable after all. When reading old books (or any books for that matter), we need to be aware of how they became the real touchable object between our hands, and what our intentions are behind how we choose to look at it.

— !!! —

Ben Blatt, however, is not the only one to neglect the involvement of editors when it comes to punctuation: Coleridge himself, attentive to such detail as he was, offered an interesting though factually faulty interpretation of a sublime passage in *Robinson Crusoe*, showing the hapless adventurer's return to the shipwreck for whatever booty that might prove useful on a tropical island. Amid essentials like forks and knives, Robinson stumbles across some coins, and launches into a sermon heard by none but him about that 'drug', money, useless in his present situation. 'However,' he lets us know, 'upon second thoughts, I took it away; and wrapping all this in a piece of canvas I began to think of making another raft.' The rawness of Crusoe's circumstances runs up against the automatic pulls of old habits of thought, a friction that pervades the novel.

Coleridge rhapsodises upon the genius of the punctuation: 'Worthy of Shakespeare; and yet the simple semicolon after it, the instant passing on without the least pause of reflex consciousness is more exquisite and masterlike than the touch itself.' Defoe is subtle, Coleridge believes, adding a 'meaner writer [...] would have put an "!" after "away," and have commenced a new paragraph.' That would have been too obvious a comment on the irony of Crusoe's contradictory actions. Leaving aside his unfair treatment of the !, Coleridge's comment is misguided: the semicolon was not Defoe's, but first appeared in the 1812 edition that Coleridge used, nearly one hundred years after the book's first printing. Originally, the lines contained a comma, offering a less striking half-pause. Does the truth make Coleridge's observation any less valuable or insightful? No. But what it does do is raise questions concerning how we assign literary worth, or withhold it.

— !!! —

In her Pulitzer Prize-winning play *W;t* (yes, it's on purpose), Margaret Edson dramatises the earnestness of punctilious editing and the absurdity of it in the face of hot searing life. *W;t* tells of the last weeks of middle-aged Dr Vivian Bearing, tortured by high-intensity cycles of chemotherapy against her stage four ovarian cancer. Hospital scenes that reduce Vivian to her mere body, naked and vulnerable, alternate with flashbacks of her time as a student of English literature, discovering the wit of seventeenth-century poets. She remembers an experience with her favourite professor, whom she, as a promising student, offended by choosing the supposedly wrong edition of John Donne's poems for her essay, thus producing a 'melodramatic veneer of scholarship'.

Donne never intended his poetry for printing, but produced it for a select circle of private readers who copied it by hand like the precious object of possession it was. We have several manuscripts of varying degrees of closeness to the originals, and a printed edition of his poems produced

Cynthia Nixon in the 2012 Broadway revival of *W;t*.

in 1633, two years after Donne's death. While Vivian used a modern edition, her professor claims the only reliable, because scholarly screened, edition is that by Helen Gardner, based on the Westmoreland manuscript of 1610. Detail matters yet again, and it matters that Vivian's female professor was educated by the female scholar she cites.

The piece Vivian analysed is part of the *Holy Sonnets*, a collection of poems on the individual's relationship to God, characterised by intense romantic or sexual love, fear, doubt, trust and hope for redemption after death. The sonnets translate a mind that is wrestling with over-whelming emotions, theological riddles and the gap between knowing this life and not knowing the other. Death, the speaker suggests, will himself die, because of our final Christian resurrection. 'In the edition you chose,' Vivian's professor berates her, 'this profoundly simple meaning is sacrificed to hysterical punctuation':

> And Death – *capital D* – shall be no more – *semicolon!* Death – *capital D* – *comma* –thou shalt die – *exclamation mark!*

The semicolon is too precious, the exclamation mark too brash and triumphant for the professor, who wryly mocks Vivian with 'if you go in for this sort of thing, I suggest you take up Shakespeare'. According to her, the text Vivian should have used reads in a more understated way: 'And death shall be no more, *comma,* Death thou shalt die.'

She continues:

> Nothing but a breath – a comma – separates life from life everlasting. It is very simple really. With the original punc-tuation restored, death is no longer something to act out on a stage, with exclamation marks. It's a comma, a pause [...] Life, death. Soul, God. Past, present. Not insuperable barriers, not semicolons, just a comma.

Thoroughly confused by her professor, Vivian promises to go back to the library and rewrite her essay using the

much pleasure, then from thee, much more must flowe
And soonest our best men, with thee doe goe,
Rest of theire bones, and soules delivery
Thou art slaue to fate, chaunce kings and desperate men,
And dost with poyson, warr and sicknes dwell.
And poppie or charmes, can make vs sleepe as well
And better then thy stroake, why swell'st thou then.
One short sleepe past, wee wake eternallye
And Death shall bee no more, Death thou shalt dye.

The Egerton manuscript of the *Holy Sonnets*, with a capital 'D' for both the first and second 'Death'.

'correct' edition. But that's also wrong for her teacher. While it's important to be precise, her professor specifies, this poem – all Donne's poems, and indeed his life – is about experience. Rather than the dark corridors of the library, Vivian ought to sit in the grass with her friends and enjoy the sunshine as the poet himself might have done.

Donne's work is thick with an intensity of feeling, thought and experience, and his life was marked by a refusal of custom and comfort, as the descendant of a Catholic family in a Protestant country, and the husband of his employer's niece. Her aristocratic father, furious at his daughter's secret wedding to a lowly secretary, destroyed Donne's career by making sure nobody would hire him for a decade, leaving the young family in dire straits. In spite of such worries, Donne managed to write some of the most lush poems of the English language, evocative, dense and sensual whether they think about the ecstasy of sex or knotty theological points.

Vivian does not follow her teacher's advice to do like Donne and live a little, instead she dedicates her life to scholarship, making enormous contributions to academia, but ending up in hospital without friends or family to comfort her during her illness. As her health deteriorates, she becomes a specimen for researchers, and a spectacle for us theatregoers. In the final cataclysmic moments, as her doctors frantically strive to resuscitate her to keep her as an object of scientific study, characters yell in capital letters with plenty of exclamation marks, reducing her final choices to this or that code. The patient does have one defender, though: 'She's NO CODE!' exclaims Vivian's nurse, the only person who cares to develop a personal relationship with her, watching in horror as the doctors mistreat her dying and dead body.

For those of us who do not make the same kind of space for faith in our lives as Donne, a comma is perhaps less appropriate for death than a !, carrying all the terrifying finality of ending.

— !!! —

Had ! been more common during Donne's lifetime, he and his friends might have used it in their compositions and copies of his poems. But how do we deal with texts that are even older than the Renaissance, that stem from a time when nobody was pondering whether or not to use an exclamation mark or semicolon, simply because they had not been invented yet? What do we do with a thousand-year-old literary masterpiece like *Beowulf*?

Beowulf is a long medieval poem about a hero, Beowulf, and his three big monster-fights against a murderous confusingly half-human creature called Grendel, then against Grendel's mother, who comes to avenge her son's death, and then, at the end of Beowulf's life, against a huge fire-spitting dragon crouching on a hoard of gold (yes, it's Tolkien's favourite poem). *Beowulf* is written in Old English, the early Germanic version of English, with Scandinavian influence, before the Norman invasion of 1066 brought French and Latin words and structures. The anonymous poem exists in a single manuscript copied between the tenth and eleventh centuries by two different scribes, who may or may not have composed the piece.

We just don't know if *Beowulf* is a transcription of orally performed and transmitted poetry, or was conceived from the start as a written document that deliberately sounds like it's an oral performance. What we do know is that the manuscript has suffered badly since its creation a millennium ago. In fact, it's a miracle it exists at all: once its value had been noticed in the sixteenth century by scholar pioneers, the book was kept in the possession of Sir Robert Cotton, whose vast book collection provided the basis of the British Library. Sadly, some of its holdings were ravaged by fire in 1731, among them the *Beowulf* manuscript. Edges singed, brittle parchment crumbling, *Beowulf* is a delicate and unique witness to the thriving cultural life of Anglo-Saxon England.

During the nineteenth century, native (rather than classical) literature became of greater interest to scholars, who researched and published folk and fairy tales such as

The opening page of the British Library's *Beowulf* manuscript, singed in a fire in the eighteenth century.

the collections of the Brothers Grimm. *Beowulf*, too, became accessible to academics (and the odd amateur reader), initiating a steady trickle of scholarly editions of the Old English text, as well as translations into modern English. How does one treat a text that is not in another language, but simply an older version of the same language, alien yet strangely familiar? What do we do with the punctuation? Is it legitimate to add marks that were not yet around at the time the poem was written down?

Anglo-Saxon scholar Eric Weiskott thinks not. Picking a particularly juicy bone with the (to him unlawful) addition of ! into *Beowulf* texts, he makes an impassioned case for the naked edition, that is, offering as few punctuation crutches as possible. In his 2012 article 'Making *Beowulf* Scream', he identifies a predilection for abundant !s during the editions of the late 1800s, followed by a sharp decline in the course of the later twentieth century. The influential 1922 edition by Frederick Klaeber adds 56 exclamation marks to the Old English words, shrinking to 7 marks by the time of the landmark Bruce Mitchell edition of 1998. As early as 1914, Weiskott argues, expert voices, such as A.J. Wyatt, were lobbying to strip out inauthentic accretions: 'our modern meretricious marks of exclamation', as Wyatt denounced them. In his typically wry tone, Wyatt concludes: if 'the reader's sense or emotions do not tell him where he ought to feel exclamatory, he must suffer the consequences'.

But it's not all that easy, since the poem itself does its best to keep us suspended in constant inference about motivations and metaphors. While it is true that semicolons and parentheses provide subtle and perhaps too subtle pauses for the style of writing from a thousand years ago, Weiskott is a little too harsh on the poor exclamation mark, calling it 'excitable', 'screechy' and 'frenetic'. A 'purely theatrical flourish'. In a provocative side-jab at our !!!-happy internet age, Weiskott decrees that 'exclamation marks are typographical equivalents of junk food: never appropriate, always alluring'. It satisfies our appetite, but it doesn't actually make us full, and it's bad for our (mental) health. The ! is superfluous, he argues. It's dirty and ugly, and has nothing to do with our solemn and stately *Beowulf*.

Beowulf was messy and full of holes, however, even before the bookworms and library fire ate through its sheets. Scribes have scratched out and changed letters here and there, loose story ends dangle out of the poem's imagined edges, and the whole thing is about a pagan society that peculiarly behaves according to Christian codes of ethics, featuring a middle-aged stay-at-home mum who goes berserk and shows herself to be a formidable foe to a dashing young warrior. That's a lot of drama for a story which isn't supposed to need expressive punctuation.

Instead of !, Weiskott proposes, we should return to the original's handful of capital letters, a dot here and there and (thankfully) spaces between words. Students may pore over the page and parse clauses whichever way makes sense. As long as there is 'verifiable syntactic data', the editor may place a discreet mark of punctuation.

But what about feeling? And when is a feeling verifiable and (dare we say it) legitimate? It seems ! makes some scholars nervous, straying as it does into the *terra incognita* of interpretation, emotion, the feminine, the uncontrolled. Very much not what *Beowulf* the poem-hero-tradition-artefact seems to be. Or is it? What about this version?

> Bro! Tell me we still know how to
> talk about kings! In the old days,
> everyone knew what men were:
> brave, bold, glory-bound. Only
> stories now, but I'll sound the
> Spear-Danes' song, hoarded for
> hungry times.

American writer Maria Dahvana Headley's modern English version of the poem, published in 2020, shatters whatever assumptions we might have of a *Beowulf* that's boring and irrelevant. Deliberately urban, over-the-top and obscene (heroes are 'fucked by fate'), with a generous injection of World Wide Web lingo ('hashtag-blessed'), Headley brilliantly updates the medieval story to our globalised social-media-impacted realities. Megalomaniac men, she contends in her introduction, still make foolish decisions for us, just as in Dark-Aged Geatland. Headley understands *Beowulf* as 'the kind of thing meant to be shouted over a crowd of drunk celebrants'. Its internal soundscape is 'a dazzling, furious, funny, vicious, desperate, hungry, beautiful, mutinous, maudlin, supernatural, rapturous shout'.

And which mark could encapsulate all of those jostling contradictory impressions better than !. Craftswoman that she is, Headley knows how to wield her exclamation: the poem's end coincides with the life of the man that conferred it its name as he fights, alone, against a smouldering dragon. The hero perishes. His band of retainers celebrate him in kind:

> They remembered the right words. Our king!
> Lonely ring-wielder! Inheritor of everything!
> He was our man, but every man dies.
> Here he is now! Here our best boy lies!
> He rode hard! He stayed thirsty! He was the man!
> He was the man.

Eight exclamation marks on six lines lift the solemnly ceremonious tone worthy of a great warrior's demise, the very last line shorn of the upwards-pointing shape of !. We bow our punctuation heads to the hero. Dust to dust.

— !!! —

Editing and writing are activities based on trust. But the small things orchestrating that activity are more vulnerable than other elements, suffering too much change, or not enough. Some writers consider their commas and colons so intrinsic to their work that they have recourse to tricks and strategies to forestall editorial intrusion. Because her publishers kept changing her punctuation, American writer and teacher Muriel Rukeyser allegedly stamped the margins of her manuscripts in red-inked directions before sending them off to print, impressing her admonishing presence onto the papers: 'PLEASE

Amanda Gorman reading at the Biden inauguration, 2021.

BELIEVE THE PUNCTUATION'. Rukeyser was a Jewish feminist fighter for social justice, and held firm to the conviction that poetry is at the heart of democracy, but that her native US had a fear of poetry, and thus of feeling. This fear leads to a devaluation of culture, eventually resulting in the ultimate negation of culture, war.

Rukeyser, one imagines, would have been delighted to witness the prominence poetry claimed during the inauguration of the 46th president of the United States, which saw Amanda Gorman, a young black poet and activist, performing her work on America's divided present and the healing task ahead, making headlines around the world. In her essay 'The Life of Poetry', Rukeyser contends the punctuation is 'measured rest. Space on the page. Eye's discernment of pattern.' It has a structuring function,

> # THE TRUTH OF A POEM IS ITS FORM AND ITS CONTENT, ITS MUSIC AND ITS MEANING ARE THE SAME.
>
> ## - MURIEL RUKEYSER -

tracking time, allocating attention. But, she says, punctuation is also 'biological'. It's the 'physical indication of the body – rhythms which the reader is to acknowledge'.

Punctuation is vocal cords; is eyes darting from comma to comma, focus gathering at the twinned half-moons of a parenthesis. Punctuation is the belly lifting and sinking with air drawn in, air expelled. Punctuation is heartbeat; coordination of limbs; coordination of consciousness.

Oh!

Ah!

Breathing. Sighing. Exclaiming.

— !!! —

The poetry of Gerard Manley Hopkins is alive with heaving, pulsating, muscular movement. The only way to express the sheer jubilant joy for the astonishing beauties of nature is to express breath, catapulted by that jack-in-the-box !. Hopkins's poem 'The Windhover' imagines a kestrel surfing the air, seemingly pinned to nothing, then swooping and swerving, being perfect in being itself.

This is strange poetry. Hopkins himself thought it so, admitting in a letter to his closest friend, 'no doubt my poetry errs on the side of oddness'. Hopkins had excelled in his studies of Greek and Latin at Oxford (he was nicknamed the 'star of Balliol'), converted to Catholicism, and as a Jesuit priest created opulent poetry. Grappling with these seemingly contradictory activities, Hopkins must also have thought himself 'odd' as a priest with homoerotic tendencies, which he kept hidden in his private writings in a late nineteenth-century England that publicly

The Windhover:

to Christ our Lord

I caught this mórning morning's mínion, king-
    dom of daylight's dauphin, dapple-dáwn-drawn Falcon, in his
        riding
Of the rólling level únderneáth him steady aír, and stríding
Hígh there, how he rung upon the rein of a wimpling wing
In his écstasy! then off, off forth on swing,
    As a skate's heel sweeps smooth on a bow-bend: the hurl and
        gliding
Rebuffed the bíg wind. My heart in hiding
Stírred for a bird,—the achieve of, the mástery of the thing!

Brute beauty and valour and act, oh, air, pride, plúme, here
    Buckle! AND the fire that breaks from thee then, a billion
Tímes told lovelíer, more dangerous, O my chevalier!

No wónder of it: shéer plód makes plóugh down síllion
Shíne, and blue-bleak embers, ah my dear,
    Fall, gáll themsélves, and gásh góld-vermílion.

punished Oscar Wilde for his sexual orientation. Perhaps channelling his feelings of apartness, Hopkins found solace and delight in observations of nature, God's gorgeous creation, its vibrant sensuous reality. Finding the tools of the poetry of his late Victorian-time not adequate for his purposes, he developed what he called 'sprung rhythm', a unique way of stressing and organising his words (the accents over the vowels are his). He was a craftsman poet, working and reworking his pieces, paying particular attention to details of sound and sight, negotiated by punctuation.

Exclamation marks migrate in and out of Hopkins's poems. Making a word leap off the page, they cluster after content-less human sounds, sighs and wonderings. As if

'The Windhover', early summer 1877. Note the exclamation mark on the penultimate line (after 'wind') which will later disappear.

forced to express by an otherworldly power, 'oh!' often violently interrupts the line, as it does in a poem celebrating the Baroque composer Henry Purcell: 'let him oh! with his air of angels'.

Literary scholar Peter Milward has attempted to pick apart the different situations of exclaiming with 'o', 'oh' and 'ah' in Hopkins's works. Is there a difference between 'ah' and 'o(h)'? 'Ah' sounds 'sharp, intense', Milward suggests, 'oh' is 'clearly more relaxed', he finds, 'with less pursing of the lips and more letting out of breath'. And, although Milward himself admits that Hopkins's use of this or that vowel is more 'erratic' than systematic, the research question doesn't matter much any more, as the scholar himself is swept away by the power of sighed exclaiming: halfway into an interpretation, he interrupts his academic composure, shouting 'this is altogether extraordinary!'. The poet is astonished at creation, and we are astonished at the poet being astonished. The best way to praise God's marvellous work is to praise it, exclaiming with wordless breath. Today, we would perhaps say 'wow!'.

— !!! —

Gerard Manley Hopkins died from typhoid fever, aged 44. His legacy remains as of a man acutely attuned to the loveliness of life, forever chasing the truest words and most immediate punctuation. One generation later, on the other side of the Atlantic, another poet picks at language, prising apart its boundaries, shaking up the contents and stitching those fragments back together again. Edward

Estlin Cummings, more widely known as e e cummings, made that which is familiar unfamiliar by dissecting words to their constituent parts, sometimes lovingly attaching this letter to that mark of punctuation, sometimes rudely shoving together unlikely sparring partners, leaving the reader wondering how to pronounce the poem, if at all.

> **(fea**
> **therr**
> **ain**
>
> **:dreamin**
> **g field o**
> **ver forest &;**
>
> **wh**
> **o could**
> **be**
>
> **so**
> **!f!**
> **te**
>
> **r?n**
> **oo**
> **ne)**

What might this poem speak about?

Would it do it justice to spell it out? Demystifying the sacred relationship between 'feather' and 'rain'? So much 'therr' on the blank page, the same shape, a drop, longish, slender, delicate contours on which the eyes slide down, safely contained by the brackets at its head and tail, suddenly exploding into its constituent sounds with the stringent exclamation mark: double !! detonate the plosive power of 'f' on the lips once it stands alone without its softening neighbours. How something so gentle can easily be tweaked into something much less so, and then again sink into evanescent questioning – who could be softer? No one? Noon? The visceral visual landscape of cummings's little gem-like carvings of poems explore and exploit the full possibilities of punctuation to connect and to divide, to make beautiful and to make unfamiliar, and both, one because of the other.

However fretful and anxious the prescriptions that grammar books try to impose, ! in the wild shows the rather different picture of a world of words and stories only too happy to exclaim, to sob, to moan, howl, holler, bellow, and also to feel. If in doubt, always believe the punctuation. Always believe the flaming pink scarf.

CHAPTER FOUR

Oi!!!

Perking up with punctuation

It's bristly. It's yellow. And it's as tall as you.
What is it?

This is not a joke, but a piece of art worth $150,000. There's a big round ball at the bottom, slightly flat perhaps, slightly outsized in comparison to the long top-hat-like teardrop floating exactly above its centre, suspended from the ceiling. The thing's surface looks fuzzy, evaporating into the ambient air at its edges, and making you blink as if you were myopic, constantly having to focus, and focus again. Most obvious of all, its colour, a glaring garish yellow, an exploded tennis ball, a splash of smoke, signalling 'here be fire'. Here be life.

It's an exclamation mark.

It's art.

Chartreuse, the title reads. A grandchild of the late-ABBA-glam-early-punk 1980s, when its creator became obsessed about punctuation. Made from rubberised horse-hair and yellow paint, in the year 2008, this is a sculpture by Richard Artschwager, American artist and furniture designer. Artschwager certainly was a man of his time, creating artworks that consisted of a single object, an

Richard Artschwager, *Exclamation Point (Chartreuse)*, 2008 © ARS, NY and DACS, London 2022.

everyday thing such as a couch, or a table, often made from synthetics such as Formica, the quintessential 1960s material. Like his contemporaries Warhol and Lichtenstein, Artschwager was a pop artist, seeking to interrogate the nature of art by pushing at the boundaries between the museum environment and the domestic.

Rethinking not only theoretical but also physical barriers, Artschwager disrupted the museum/city divide by scattering what he called blps (pronounced as 'blips') – white rectangular strips the size of a palm – onto walls, delivery trucks, industrial chimneys or shop windows. These lozenges (which he self-mockingly called a 'longitudinal cross-section of a knackwurst') instantly transformed the thing thus tattooed, infusing it with the possibility of being apprehended for more than its customary and necessary function.

Inspired by explorations of the role of emptiness in art (think of John Cage's 4'33"), Artschwager married his blps with silence, creating a series of punctuation mark sculptures between 1966 and 1990. Series after series of differently sized ! and ? and ' ' dominated Artschwager's exhibitions: standing, suspended, attached to the wall, wood or rubber, fuzzy, hard, sometimes vague, always tactile 3D distillations of formerly flat textual markers. Adam Weinberg of the Whitney Museum of American Art said that 'they appear as humorous, sensuous forms, yet mute ones, detached from their dramatic feeling or sound that they would imply in a text.' Though exiled from their natural habitat, Artschwager's decontextualised punctuation marks still retain their striking affective potential: still inject hesitation when encountered reeling freely in the gallery, perhaps even more so than when moored by words. Words offer a semblance of control – what exactly is it you are quoting, you are shouting about? Stumbling across ! without anchor can be a fearsome experience.

Punctuation marks do something to us, with or without letters. They do something to the space around them, punctuating it, summoning and recruiting it into their effect. Space becomes apprehensible, a foil, a photo negative of the solid thing against which it presses. In the same way that sculpted punctuation marks choreograph the construction of space in the gallery, textual signs organise the wildly blank prairie of the page. Artschwager, in a manner, realises in sculpture what e e cummings worked towards in poetry, the loosening of conventionally locked things, characters or ideas, presenting them as starkly themselves.

There's something special about !, though. It's not for nothing that Artschwager calls it the 'prince of punctuation'. In the gallery, the exclamation mark stands alone, but it's not lonely: it 'can operate with respect to itself or anybody/thing around', Artschwager notes, adding it's 'spiralling free but gravity-aware. Hopping on one foot .:.' What attracted Artschwager is both the form of ! – the grounded dot, the body suspended, circular and upright at the same time – and its provocative power to make a cultural statement. Does it represent our noisy times? Is it a middle finger to conventional art, to those slashing arts funding? It's serious and goofy at the same time.

Although we don't know what Artschwager's ! is exclaiming about, it sure has exclamatory weight. It is what designer Martin Solomon calls a 'full-bodied' mark, a 'major' one, 'very loud (*fortissimo*)', regardless of the words it attaches to and amplifies. Classifying textual punctuation marks according to musical value, Solomon thinks they are the 'heartbeat of typography, moving words along in proper timing and with proper emphasis'. But they also 'have mass and energy': punctuation, he contin- ues, 'is to typography what perspective is to painting. It introduces the illusion of visual and audible dimension, giving words vitality.' Punctuation immerses us in experi- ence. It is experience.

It's not clear why ! looks like it does: its inventor Alpoleio describes the shape, but doesn't tell us how he got the idea. Perhaps it was because the wordish equiva- lent of wonder is the Latin *io*, something like 'hurray'. One can imagine how, hastily scribbled one on top of the

! – Calibri

! – Garamond

! – Helvetica

! – Times New Roman

! – ALGERIAN

! – Bauhaus

! in different fonts ... though nobody would scream in Helvetica, of course.

other, 'o' becomes a dot migrating to the bottom of the line, and i swirling towards the top. Perhaps a stacked 'i-o' represents the collapsed first and last letters of *interiectio* (interjection). But 'wow' sounds more appropriate for the admirable point.

It just seems that there's something about the circle and the vertical stroke, held together in creative tension by an invisible bridge, that catches our eye, and makes us sit up. ! in a museum piques our interest. ! in a text grabs our attention, whether we want it to or not.

— !!! —

In 1956, German sociologist and philosopher Theodor Adorno likened the exclamation mark to 'soundless clashing of cymbals', a '*sforzato*' surprise of noise, also to a traffic sign (red, of course). Adorno doesn't like the exclamation mark at all: it has become 'corrupted into a claim of importance' it doesn't legitimately have, when the writer leans on its sensational flashiness to generate interest. Sound and fury, but no substance. Expressionist writers of the post-First World War era overused !, turning it into the punctuational equivalent of 'the million numbers on the bank notes of German inflation'.

Worse than simple over-abundance, however, was what Adorno saw as !'s 'unbearable gesture of authority'. Amid the anatomy of punctuation marks, ! is 'an index finger raised in warning'. Watch out!, the exclamation mark seems to say. Do this, but don't do that! One can understand Adorno's dislike for the authoritarian !,

113

considering his experience of racial abuse, contempt for his academic work, and Nazi-imposed exile. Yet it's undeniable that ! grabs us and shakes us into paying attention, telling us something important has happened, or is about to.

— !!! —

It makes perfect sense that befuddled comic characters show their amazement with a speech bubble, empty but for the confused '?', followed by an emphatic '!' when they understand.

The lettering of comics is crucial to their aesthetics, exaggerating shapes and colours, and encoding over-sized verbal sound effects with an extra-exclamation-mark-

Suddenly everything is obvious!

Irv Novick's original comic book panel from DC Comics' *All-American Men of War*, which Roy Lichtenstein adapted.

oomph. Historians of the genre suggest that the high volume of **!** in comics can be traced to their early days at the beginning of the twentieth century, when printing was a somewhat slapdash affair. Making sure that a line of text would have a final punctuation mark once printed, letterers would use an exclamation rather than a full stop, because the full stop was more likely to lose colour during the inking process. This practical solution nicely coheres with the energy and emotionally charged stories of comics, and it was this mixture of strong visuals and intense feeling that attracted pop artists like Roy Lichtenstein to appropriate the styles and images of comic culture, bringing what was perceived as juvenile and frivolous into highbrow museums and money-pushing art auctions.

Lichtenstein's 1963 *Whaam!* shows a fighter pilot unleashing fire on an enemy plane. He had lifted the motif wholesale from a panel created just a year earlier by comic artist Irv Novick, justifying the move as a critique of that particular kind of American aggression in Vietnam. The picture was supposed to shake viewers into consciousness.

Irv Novick, meanwhile, remained unacknowledged and uncompensated, and was struggling to make ends meet. The first owners of *Whaam!* sold it to the Tate Gallery for nearly £4,000 in 1966, a considerable sum at the time. Now, it's worth millions. ! can make us aware of injustice, but it cannot cure it.

— !!! —

What writers and artists have known all along has now been substantiated by science: Utrecht sociology professor Kees Van Den Bos has researched the function of ! on human attention and decision-making, finding that participants who had been shown an image of an exclamation mark thought faster and judged more severely. An MRI machine was used to measure activity in different areas of the brain as participants looked at a screen that showed texts describing ethical situations of varying (in)justice, before being asked to judge how fair the scenario seemed to them. Before some of the scenarios, the screen would flash a warning diamond with ! at its centre, after which participants labelled the outcome offered to the situation to be 'very unfair' rather than just 'unfair'. What's more, participants responded faster to the task of assessing, and reported that they felt more alert after seeing the exclamation mark (as opposed to a question mark, for example, introduced among other control stimuli). The computer corroborated what the participants reported, attesting to a greater neural activity in the medial pre-frontal cortex, where our brains process alarming and emotion-heavy information.

Kees Van Den Bos flashes a warning sign.

Van Den Bos concluded that ! primes us to pay attention: this is not panicking, but the stage before, when we try to determine if what's in front of us is worth getting worried over. Because the energy we need for attention is costly, evolution has made sure that there are several hoops we need to jump through before getting into gear and running away or fighting: the exclamation mark lifts us into the first stage of analysis, making us decide whether to pay closer attention or not. Seeing a ! speeds up brain processes and flags up potentially dangerous situations. Whether that's inherent in its shape, or something we've acquired through encountering exclamation marks in texts or as symbols of 'beware' in our daily life, its agency over us remains the same. We perk up as if someone had pinched us.

─ !!! ─

But it's not only our minds upon which ! leaves its mark: when we read, our brain sends tiny signals to our vocal cords, which contract imperceptibly as if we were truly speaking. Scientists have detected electrical activity in the larynx and muscles involved in articulation of speech, a charge so minimal that consciousness does not register it, yet enough to produce a feedback loop in the mind: 'subvocalisation' increases working memory, the part of memory which holds streams of incoming impressions in an accessible and malleable state, integrating new experiences and aiding comprehension. Punctuation helps feel the rhythm of a sentence, and so contributes to our internal sense of sound. Punctuation primes our bodies, which prime our minds. The more we subvocalise, linguists like Elizabeth Schotter argue, the better our memory and our processing of what we read.

It would be foolish and fatal to the purpose of reading – understanding and keeping information – to suppress that voice in our heads, but that's exactly what speed readers attempt to do. They also try to eliminate eye movement (that is, the eye methodically working its way through a text) by using a device called a tachistoscope which has single words flash on a screen in rapid sequence, never lingering, never repeating, never actually moving, but jogging in one place. Reading through such a device, however, is counterproductive, operating in opposition to intuitive assumptions; the eye is not gliding from letter to letter or word to word, but rather leaps ahead eight or nine letters (to the right if the text is written in a Western language). It fixates on a letter or a punctuation mark, then parcels together a bunch of letters, before jumping ahead to the next fixation point. Fixation takes 225 milliseconds (that's a quarter of a second); those froggy leaps ('saccades') are faster still, catapulting focus within 50 milliseconds. The letters before and after the fixation point are blurry, but our eyes are still capable of grasping their shape and making sense. Young readers hop fewer letters, and need to circle back and reread more often, but even skilled speed readers regress around 15 per cent of the time.

So, when one reads each individual word as a brief apparition on a screen, immediately followed by another and another and another, reading speed may nominally increase, but memory retention will not. In fact, working memory will be bogged down the same way as when we suppress subvocalisation. Flashing words also don't allow for regression, and there's no software to predict just when exactly our brains need our eyes to return and re-read. It turns out that our brains fixate intelligently and our vocal cords twitch for a reason. The best way to read is to read the way we do naturally. The best way to read faster in one area of knowledge is to read similar texts, since familiarity increases speed, because we expect certain words and phrases, and not others.

Maybe Woody Allen said all that needs to be said on the topic: 'I've been doing a speed-reading course. It's great. Last Friday night, I read all of *War and Peace*. [Pause.] It's about Russia.'

— !!! —

Letter shape and arrangement also affect our eye's ability to decipher and process: English has its identifying features in the top halves of letters, making the top sample below by Renan Gross decipherable, while the lower one (with just the bottom halves of letters) is less so.

High contrast between letter forms and sizes increases discernible difference, and thus readability. THIS IS MORE DIFFICULT TO READ than this. As our eyes travel up and down the mountain range of words, the sequence of peaks and valleys produces desirable difficulty: just enough contrast to tease our eye into curiosity, but not too much jagged business to turn us off. ! is a key player in the visual symphony of highs and lows, lifting any too-orderly line of text into a bonanza of difference.

The speed and strength of our comprehension of a text also depends on our general mood, the page's design and the text's typeface, our intention towards the text (what do

Call me Ishmael. Some years ago—never mind
how long precisely—having little or no money in
my purse, and nothing particular to interest me
on shore, I thought I would sail about a little and
see the watery part of the world.

_____

Call me Ishmael. Some years ago—never mind
how long precisely—having little or no money in
my purse, and nothing particular to interest me
on shore, I thought I would sail about a little and
see the watery part of the world.

Moby Dick upper and lower, from computer scientist Renan Gross's blog, 'Sarcastic Resonance'.

we seek to get from it?), our surroundings (reading in a noisy coffee shop?) and our availability (are we multi-tasking?). Emotion, anatomy and design come together in a trio of function: ! is indispensable for the full-bodied, fully felt, fully thought experience that is reading.

The best writers can work magic with a well-placed !, enhancing our physical sensation of what we read. Too often, though, the might of ! gets abused, turning punctuation into a handmaid of brainwashing, social division and destructive consumption. The exclamation mark's alertness effect has been exploited by advertising agencies online and offline, whose branding and logos often end on !, although it may be seen as crude and overly chummy. Symantec cyber security finds that email spam rides the wave of the exclamation mark's power to create a sense of urgency: ! tails five out of the six most used words in email spam, including 'fingertips!', 'online!', 'here!', and 'today!'. Only 'available' remains without this punctuation appendix, perhaps because it's too long and wordy. ! makes us sit up, and get ready for what comes next, and it's exactly this built-in booming siren on which business and politics capitalise in their race for our attention.

Marshall McLuhan, the first mass media sociologist, argued that the way in which we receive a message alters the way we think and perceive. The medium is the message, he says, and it was to be the title of his most famous book – although a printer's typo inspired him to leave it as the punning *The Medium is the Massage*. We might want to adjust a little: *! is the message.*

CHAPTER FIVE

Radiating punctuation: Exclamatory politics and the nuclear bomb

It's everywhere. Coffee mugs, postcards, shirts, tote bags, key chains. The red background, the restrained no-frills white letters, the iconic stylised crown hovering above words that seem to express something quintessentially British, or at least what the world thinks is quintessentially British, or some Brits do: KEEP CALM AND CARRY ON. The stiff upper lip when catastrophe strikes. During the last years of the 2000s, the slogan and its distinctive visual style conquered the globe, regenerating itself again and again in innumerable variations: a reversed complementary NOW PANIC AND FREAK OUT; a festive KEEP CALM AND HO HO HO; a KEEP CALM AND PRESS CRTL+ALT+DEL for the computer nerd; and, of course, during the pandemic, the inevitable WEAR A MASK AND

CARRY ON. Sometimes other icons replace the crown, from a gun to a mobile phone. Sometimes the background changes colour or pattern. KEEP CALM AND CARRY ON is perhaps the most successful meme since the invention of the internet.

Remarkably, we owe its existence to an odd slice of luck. In 2000, Stuart Manley, owner of Barter Books, a secondhand bookshop in Northumberland, bought a box of volumes at an auction, and discovered an old poster inside it. He liked it, gave it a nice frame and put it up behind his till. A steady trickle of customers asked to buy it, so (the copyright having expired) he had 50 prints made, which quickly sold out. Manley sold an ever-increasing number of posters, until, five years after his original find, the *Guardian* published an article about it. Demand exploded, and the poster had gained worldwide traction by 2009, when it crossed the Atlantic in the wake of the financial crisis.

The Ministry of Information's trio of reassuring posters for wartime Britain. A bit of a flop at the time.

The call to stoic resilience in the face of disaster was born in 1939, when the British government created a trio of posters to boost the morale of the British public at the beginning of the Second World War. 'FREEDOM IS IN PERIL, DEFEND IT WITH ALL YOUR MIGHT', 'YOUR COURAGE, YOUR CHEERFULNESS, YOUR RESOLUTION, WILL BRING US VICTORY', and 'KEEP CALM AND CARRY ON'.

The first two designs found their way onto walls and billboards. KEEP CALM was held in reserve for possible invasion of Britain by Nazi Germany, when alleviating panic would be the order of the day. That invasion never happened, but the public didn't take to the siblings at all: they were too wordy, and too patronising. And anyway, the British didn't want to be told what to feel, but what to do. After the flop of the first two posters, KEEP CALM never made it into the public sphere, in spite of its huge production costs (around £3 million in today's money). Most of the specimens were pulped and recycled, with paper being in short supply as the war went on.

At the time, the designs had been a new form of poster art. The British Ministry of Information enlisted help from London Transport, who had created the city's tube maps, and were at the cutting edge of typographic design. Today, with distance, in different circumstances, we appreciate the sleek style. During the war, though, people needed something else. Nazi Germany quickly figured out an effective propaganda aesthetic that gave people clear orders, through images and lettering and appealing to the emotions. The exclamation mark was one of the tools for grabbing attention and shaking the nervous system. War needs !

German encouragement to cover the windows at night ('The enemy sees your light! Black out!') and a simpler graphic exclamation from the British.

Countries on all sides followed suit and developed the art of the propaganda poster, a sophisticated interaction of word and image with punctuation pushing people into alertness. The British, too, eventually opted for unusual hurry and emotional emphasis, replacing 'KEEP CALM' with an urgent 'GO TO IT!'. The letters' edges dissolve from the very speed with which they are rushing into action, the short two-letter red-on-white words running diagonally across the page, pulled out of the frame by the declarative confident !. No more steadiness: we need to act, and act now!

When mobilisation rather than a level head is called for during wartime, the 'KEEP CALM' slogan, shorn naked of punctuation, doesn't work. But it does work for us today, seeking some of the poster's cool deliberation. One could argue that a full stop after 'CARRY ON' would create a

Exclamation mark war! 'Rosie the Riveter' (left) was the most recognisable US poster (later adopted by feminists in the fight for equal work rights). The Italian propaganda poster –'Those are the "liberators"!'– uses quotation marks to mock Allies' claims of bringing freedom while destroying hospitals and ancient buildings.

stabilising point of rest for the eye, allowing a pause to let the words sink in. On the other hand, 'CARRY ON' suggests continuation, not stagnation. In that sense, it's a smart choice to relinquish that final closing dot.

— !!! —

Punctuation's quiet power to influence minds and feelings also impacts modern choices for an electoral logo. Campaigning for a second term in office in 2012, Barack Obama opted for a slogan of white letters on petrol-blue ground with the signature 'O' logo filled by fertile red-and-white-striped American fields, under the white sun of dawn, rising into the Democratic blue sky. Obama's 'O'; one word; one period. 'FORWARD.'.

Obama's first campaign tags in 2008 had been the equally monosyllabic 'HOPE' and 'CHANGE' and 'PROGRESS'. Note the lack of punctuation for those. 'HOPE' and 'CHANGE' swirl with energy and future potential; they can't get entrapped by punctuation. Upwards and onwards. Four years later, however, it's no longer about lofty aspirations, but with continuing the good work (a second presidential term). The full stop in the 2012 slogan makes sense, but it can seem like slamming the brakes on and even work in contradiction to the meaning of 'FORWARD'. Legend has it, before releasing 'FORWARD', Obama's senior advisory team fought heatedly over the inclusion or exclusion of the

Obama makes a point in his re-election campaign.

What is it about the right? In his campaign for Britain's Conservative Party leadership, Rishi Sunak became *RISH!*, ditching the final letter of his name for a !. It was all a bit too slick.

punctuation mark, a debate which the president himself brought to an end, choosing the 'period' as a calming anchor for the eyes and the American soul.

Right-wing pundits picked up on the potential opposition between the full stop and the word's meaning. Yet, the punctuation does exactly what it's supposed to do, neutralising the tone, and offering rest: it's 'FORWARD', so there's some unfinished business; and there's a full stop, so this propulsion isn't to be powered by indistinct wishes, ideas and ideals, but by fortitude and determination. The same-sized all-caps provide a visual representation of stability and strength; sophisticated kerning (the space between each letter) balances out the letters. Word, design and punctuation encapsulate the perfect blend of momentum and poise. A tension that's productive, not anxiety-inducing. Imagine 'FORWARD!'. That looks more like the hurried order of a pushy personal trainer than the identifying image of the leader of a globally influential nation.

Presidential punctuation also makes headlines in other countries: Emmanuel Macron's first bid at the French presidency in 2016 had all the fresh wind of a young and unspoilt candidate whose motivational exclamation 'en marche!' encouraged voters to cast their voice beyond the traditional left/right divide for a 39-year old centrist political newbie. Seven years – and a Trump presidency, pandemic and a war in Eastern Europe – later, the heat of presidential campaigning moved up a few notches, producing !-laced slogans and new parties from the whole gamut of political disposition: from Paris's mayor and socialist candidate Anne 'Hidalgo! 2022' to the centre's Jean Lassalle and his 'RÉSISTONS!' party, the centre-right 'LIBRES!' of Valérie Pécresse, and the newly founded far right 'RECONQUÈTE!' of Éric Zemmour. Depending on perspective, the exclamation

A far-right exclamation mark from Éric Zemmour.

mark either warned of a landslide to the right, or lobbied for a supposed patriotic reclaiming of the country back to its unadulterated white roots. Exclamation-marked posters abounded, so much so that the French press called them a pandemic that was 'as contagious as the Omicron variant'. However, the initial exclaimer, incumbent president Emmanuel Macron, refrained from any such sound and fury on the campaign trail, opting for the unpunctuated slogan 'Avec vous' ('With you'), which was changed into the more inclusive 'Nous tous' ('All of us') two weeks before the second round.

One might have thought that no punctuation (or a modest full stop) would have been the choice of Macron's close ally, former German chancellor Angela Merkel, but her PR team thought otherwise. During a press conference on the 2015 refugee crisis in Europe, which saw Germany taking in a record number of nearly one million people, Merkel spoke out with uncharacteristic optimism: 'Wir schaffen das' ('We can do it' or 'We'll manage'), she said, a phrase said in her characteristically level voice that got snapped up by her media team and turned into the over-enthusiastic 'WIR SCHAFFEN DAS!', a proclamation that graced party posters and websites for months.

It prompted plenty of riffs from supporters and opponents alike, ranging from the stirring 'WIR MÜSSEN DAS SCHAFFEN!' ('We have to manage it!') and the doubtful 'SCHAFFEN WIR DAS?' ('Are we managing it?') to the right wing's predictably negative 'WIR SCHAFFEN DAS NICHT!' ('We aren't managing it!'). Perhaps the phrase would have received a little less attention and become less representative of the divisions of German society developing that year if that **!** had not been attached to Merkel's unexclaimed statement.

— !!! —

Punctuation (and exclamation marks) can both help or hinder a political campaign. Jeb Bush, one of the US 2016 presidential contenders, attempted to capitalise on ! with far less success. In the run-up to the Republican candidate selection, Jeb, George Bush's second son, faced heat from commentators for enthusiastically slapping ! after his name, making it 'sound like a Broadway musical'.

The exclamation mark's energy cannot make a bad sign good. Graphic designer Sagi Haviv commented on the overbearing tone of *Jeb!*: 'I'll decide if I get excited.'

Usually, political logos are custom-made by top designers, translating into visual form the essence of a candidate. Jeb's logo, by contrast, was in an old-fashioned font, Baskerville, available to anyone working in Word. That made **Jeb!** look worn out (and indeed, he had been using

a version of the logo since his first run at Florida governor in 1994). Critics also claimed the logo confused the eye with its unequal scaling of its elements: the date is too small, the ! too big in relation to the Jeb name. There's neither proportionate harmony, nor intriguing contrast. It's a bit boring, reflecting unhappily on its 'owner'. Milton Glaser – the designer who created the iconic 'I♥NY' – believes the candidate's team opted for the ! in order to 'generate a sense of enthusiasm and excitement', because 'Jeb doesn't seem to be a personality who achieves that goal, so you kind of have to invent it for him.'

Glaser also suggests Jeb might have wanted the exclamation mark to subsume his surname, a name tainted by the warmongering of the old Bush dynasty. The exclamation mark has to do double duty, faking conviction for a wishy-washy candidate who himself lacks commitment to anything, and paradoxically hiding his origins. At best, *Jeb!* felt bossy, forcing its excitement on the voters. At worst, its out-of-kilter shouting sent out forebodings of lacklustre but hysterical conservatism.

During the run-up to the Republican primaries between February and June 2016, Steven Colbert exercised his wit over the *!* in *Jeb!* again and again: he mocked the apparent disjunction between the mark's infusion of energy and excitement, and Bush's colourless public personality. Colbert proposed he should 'explore other punctuation-based emotions', such as **?** (appropriate for the man who doesn't know what he stands for), or **;** because 'it's smart, but you're not sure what it does, or where it belongs'. His favourite was **Jeb***, since it 'would create curiosity. Then people could check the footnotes and see "yep, he's still running for president"'.

— ! ! ! —

While we can afford not to take *Jeb!* too seriously, the same can't be said for the punctuation politics of another Republican, whose abuse of the exclamation mark has added fuel to its detonating power over our consciousness. Just five days after Obama won his second term in November 2012, a New York business mogul trade-marked an exclamatory slogan that would haunt the world. In July 2015, Donald J. Trump wore the first of millions of red caps with the future slogan of his own presidential campaign, 'MAKE AMERICA GREAT AGAIN!'

The Trump campaign marketed the MAGA slogan into a multi-million-dollar industry. But, oddly enough, two other presidents had used it before him: Bill Clinton in 2008, and, going back earlier, Ronald Reagan in 1980. Reagan's presidential campaign slogan had the somewhat more inviting and less exclamatory tone: 'Let's make America great again'. Perhaps the world just wasn't ready for a political ! back then. Perhaps social media had to happen first, with its amping up of emotional volume.

The slogan may have worked perfectly for Trump, but, just like Jeb's logo, 'MAKE AMERICA GREAT AGAIN!' was a mess from a graphic designer's point of view, mixing a serif font for 'America' and sans serif for 'make great again'. The thick, vaguely modern look of the sans serif and the stately old-fashioned serif jar in more ways than

A divided America – even from a kerning perspective.

one: the space between individual letters (the kerning) is uneven, creating gaps of white that threaten to disintegrate the words. Graphic designer Martin Silvertant has analysed this, showing that the inconsistent distribution of blue on white makes the slogan come apart: 'MAKE AMERI C A GREA T AGAIN!'. It's subtle, but once you're aware of it you can't unsee it.

Aesthetically, one could say the slogan is a loser (to use the candidate's own speak); politically, of course, it proved unbelievably successful. And perhaps the fonts played their part in this, with the grand, serifed 'AMERICA' harking back to a time of white conservative supremacy, while the sans serif implied the no-frills ethos of corporate America. Those different mental time zones rubbed against one another, perfectly embodying a brand that promised to go back to the future. And, just as the clumsy lack of kerning made the slogan fall apart around its key words 'America' and 'great', the country allowed itself to fall prey to the divisive demagoguery of Trump.

But it's punctuation, rather than fonts, that concerns us. And here, too, there is friction. As if the words of the slogan hadn't already achieved maximum division, its punctuation made things even worse: 'MAKE AMERICA GREAT AGAIN!' – and the second round's 'KEEP AMERICA GREAT!' - tapped into the power of! to sneak itself into our nervous system, and keep us perpetually panicky.

And it was not just MAGA hats that contributed to that high-strung mixture of aggression and hysteria: there was also a media platform that capitalised on the human appetite for snappy titbits that promise an easy way out of complex issues. Donald Trump reached audiences well before the advent of Twitter, that is true; but it's undeniable that the digital information circulation system opened up vast new opportunities for the master loudmouth and manipulator of emotion, enlisting! as its handmaid. Digital sound bites were compounded by the workings of !, as we'll see in the next chapter.

Marshall McLuhan described the hydrogen bomb as 'history's exclamation mark', asserting that 'it ends an age-long sentence of manifest violence'. The outrageousness of nuclear weapons, he proposed, put an end to material hardware combat, ushering in an age of electronic warfare, a battle of the images, as it were, a struggle for sovereignty over information which is, eventually, a grab for our 'central nervous system' that 'electric technology' infiltrates.

CHAPTER SIX

At your fingertips
Digital !

Donald J. Trump's proclivity for the frenetic use of ! became well known soon after he travelled down that gold-shimmering escalator in Trump Tower on 16 June 2015 to announce his candidacy for the presidency. Trump's mouthpiece of choice was Twitter, a minimally supervised social media platform built on snatches of information no longer than 140 characters (since doubled).

In the run-up to nominations, statistical data journalism website FiveThirtyEight published a table showing the use of one, two, three or more !s in tweets by the respective candidates. Between November 2015 and June 2016, Republican contenders were three to six times more likely to use at least one ! in their tweets than their Democratic counterparts. An exclamation mark snuck into just 9 per cent of tweets from Bernie Sanders, and only 7 per cent from Hilary Clinton, and was close to zero for more than one exclamation mark. Ted Cruz, on the other hand, stuffed more than 30 per cent of his tweets with at least one exclamation mark, while Donald Trump showered as many as 60 per cent with at least one !, one in ten tweets with !!, and was no stranger to !!! or even !!!!.

This exclamatory compulsion did not go unnoticed: the *Washington Post* observed that, were this not the chosen nominee of the Republican Party, his words would look like 'someone on the verge of a hysterical breakdown or a profound religious awakening'. *Vogue* designated Trump's tweets 'the signature of a manic, midnight ranter', of a 'resentment-fuelled insomniac so accustomed to the amped up volume of his own thoughts that he no longer listens to anything outside of his own skull.' Is this a fair assessment of the former president and his punctuation habits? Or are those just the usual defamations levelled at ! and those bravely pushing the shift+! keys on their smartphones?

If the numbers of his !s are undeniably high, how exactly was Donald Trump using the exclamation mark? NBC News analysed Trump's words in positive and negative tweets in 2016, as well as the content of those including !, finding that ! pops up in event announcements (such as a rally), as well as dismissals or appraisals of a person, institution or idea. There's little of the exclamation mark's sense of wonder or admiration in their word cloud. Except, perhaps, 'Wow!', distinctly smaller in the map than the self-centred 'Me!', and smaller than 'Enjoy!', Trump's most frequent word-exclamation-mark-pair between February 2016 and February 2017, notably capping tweets about his own air-times.

Business news website Quartz made note of Trump's habit of using one to two-word-plus-! tweet sign-offs. 'Enjoy!' in first place is followed by a cheerful 'Thank you!', and a less friendly but trademark 'Sad!', then 'Nice!' and 'Very nice!' (#4 and #7), 'Terrible!' (#9), 'So sad!' (#13) and 'So true!' (#15).

Strong emotive words dominate the list, with moral judgments ('Disgraceful!'), intensifiers ('Very unfair!')

Trump's wordmap, as plotted by NBC News in 2016.

and imperious commands ('Apologize!'). It's as if Trump intuitively understands Van Den Bos's study on the effects of the exclamation mark on our vigilance, adeptly using the exclamation mark's manipulative might: ! switches on our cognitive alert button, a healthy response in a genuinely alarming situation in real life, a problematic one when encountered again and again in a diatribe on screens.

The appearance of ! in uncalled-for circumstances increases an anchorless sense of urgency in viewers, contributing to excessive social polarisation. Whether justified or not, Republican voters reported increased anxiety over their life and safety – diffuse notions of unrelenting angst which Trumpian rhetoric and !-happiness kept feeding.

It served Trump well to inject constant strife and over-excitement into the digital sphere through which he reached an unprecedented number of people, building a chummy rapport with followers by bypassing the established communication outlets, and serving as a mouthpiece for those who felt ignored by career politicians. In the largely lawless parallel universe of the world wide web, definitions are cut loose, sailing unmoored through murky waters of subjectively-claimed meaning. 'Fake mainstream media' and 'alternative facts' become common currency, boosted into credibility by the exclamation mark's magic.

A 2006 study, from Southern Connecticut State University, analysed the function of ! in several online messaging groups, finding that users employed the sign to emphasise supposed 'statements of fact' – statements that are, in fact, 'opinions stated as facts'. Subjective

truth-parades. Trump's Twitter had turned ! into the serv-
ant of discord, stress and post-truth dystopia. But ! balked
at this abuse.

— !!! —

Ever since its launch in 2006, Twitter has been urged by
individuals, institutions and governments to establish
some kind of regulation concerning the etiquette of what
could and could not be said. Pressure grew as Donald
Trump's candidacy and presidency highlighted the urgency
of introducing new ground rules. Twitter held off for a
long time, deflecting the charge that it was condoning
Trump's inflammatory hectoring by arguing that his posts
were 'newsworthy'. Finally, though, in the wake of the
2020 election and the torrent of misinformation around
the pandemic, Twitter had to grow a conscience, and
enlisted ! to rise to the challenge of redeeming itself and
the platform. In May 2020, the media platform added a
circled exclamation mark to flag up potential (or probable)
misinformation. By clicking on the fact-check alert, you
could read Twitter's take on the situation.

Towards the end of the year, as Trump sought a second
term as president, things hotted up. Trump had begun
tweeting, without any justification, that the election would
be rigged. Twitter offered its circled ! for readers to 'get
the facts'. And then, as Trump lost, and the inauguration of
Biden approached, ! would accelerate Trump's undoing.
The raving messages of a bad loser encouraged around
80,000 followers to gather in Washington DC, some

Donald J. Trump ✔
@realDonaldTrump

There is NO WAY (ZERO!) that Mail-In Ballots will be anything less than substantially fraudulent. Mail boxes will be robbed, ballots will be forged & even illegally printed out & fraudulently signed. The Governor of California is sending Ballots to millions of people, anyone.....

⚠ Get the facts about mail-in ballots

Twitter finally exclaims.

5,000 of whom stormed the heart of American politics, the Capitol, on 6 January 2021. Two days later, on 8 January, Trump posted the promise that the '75,000,000 great American Patriots who voted for me, AMERICA FIRST, and MAKE AMERICA GREAT AGAIN, will have a GIANT VOICE long into the future. They will not be disrespected or treated unfairly in any way, shape or form!!!'. It is easy to imagine how the spark struck by the triple exclamation mark could jump over to inflame further mobilisation, particularly since the next post informed fans that the outgoing president would boycott the inauguration of his successor. After the Capitol catastrophe, Twitter chose to pull the plug on its most famous user, and suspended Trump's account until further notice.

While Donald Trump took his predilection for ! to his own platform, Truth Social, the exclamation mark is forever (or for now) tainted with his association: online writers such as Julia Felsenthal ponder whether they can still use it, or whether we can ever unsee its recent past, as the 'punctuation equivalent of mansplaining'. Its formerly 'playful silhouette' has now become 'aggressively phallic'. So, must we resign ! to its guilty existence as textual dick pic, or can we redeem it from its abuse? Let's make ! innocent again. Again!

– !!! –

Of course, Trump is not the only person to overdo the exclamation marks: repetition of glyphs is part and parcel of digital communication. 'Yassssss', 'shiiiiiiit', 'hahahahahahaha', 😂😂😂😂😂😂 and !!!!!!!!!!!!!!!!!!! are rife in the world of upscaled internet speech. 'Argh' is no longer enough. It has to be 'argggh' or 'arggggggh'. We need to escalate, and keep escalating our words, or letters, inflating our messages to almost absurd lengths. It's noteworthy that the words or signs we kick up a notch tend to be emotional sounds, or social interactions of agreement or disagreement. Twitter's twenty most-used words confirm this increase in emotion in the digital sphere, including *ah*, *yeah*, *wow*, *really*, *ugh*, *oh*, *love*, *good*, *crazy*, *hey*, *please*, *shit*, *damn*, *mad* and *yay*. Is all this textual effusion a symptom of the degeneracy of language on the World Wide Web? Or is there a logic to the loudness?

There is a logic, of course, and it lies at the very heart of our humanity. It's because we are intensely social beings, and as such possess remarkably fine-tuned antennae for exuding, catching and interpreting cues about interpersonal information. In comparison to face-to-face talks, computer-mediated communication may seem artificial and isolating – we just need to look up from our own phone and observe all the other passengers in the train carriage staring at theirs – but they're still tools of connection. Digital media is socially oriented. As such, we need a sociology of internet language, because it's about maintaining and managing relationships, sometimes peacefully, sometimes less so (witness social media trolls). Billions of people are now just a click away, but we essentially behave as if we were still living in tribes, with all the positive and negative side effects.

The internet is basically one big gossip machine, a marketplace for voices of all sorts. We want to talk talk talk to one another, yet we have to do so in writing. 'Chatting' has acquired its written expression in the form of (supposedly) live real-time back and forth of (supposedly) spontaneous reactions. Internet text is digi-talk. It's oral-written, as it were, although we want it to function like live language. There will always be a time lag when we type rather than speak, however minuscule; we can always go back and delete what we wrote before choosing to click 'send'. Typing is thinking, sending is speaking. This sequential switching does not happen in real life. In a live conversation, we get constant feedback from our interlocutor through posture, nodding or humming, encouraging us to adapt and update our own speech and demeanour as we go along. Not so in the timing of digi-talk.

There will always be a difference between face-to-face communication and thumb-to-thumb, and it's a difference that bugs us: attempting to cross that chasm, we have developed strategies to create a semblance of liveness, a distinct genre of 'as if'. There's a tacit understanding that multiplied lettersssssss, ALL CAPS, slightlie wrng spelling, and ldkjvb (key smash) express spontaneity, 'recording speech verbatim' as internet linguist Gretchen McCulloch asserts. Textual aberrations like !!!!!!!!!!!!!! become acceptable, because they stand as a marker for improvisation. McCulloch herself, though, describes how we will often adjust our seemingly unfiltered text production before sending, substituting some letters for others, because we don't like the look of the spontaneous sequence. We can't help but edit.

At least every texter gets to be their own editor. Unlike professional text production, internet writing is volatile, boundless and in constant flux. Nobody actively maintains the web. Blogging, tweeting, commenting, updating a Facebook status, private digital messaging: billions of users establish their own ever-changing conventions through use in the biggest collective experiment humanity has ever undertaken. The internet is demotic, democratic, messy and informal, and conversational without a mouth. The internet lacks a body. This is precisely the problem.

─ !!! ─

In a 1970 sketch, Danish-American comedian Victor Borge proposed what he called 'phonetic punctuation', that is, translating punctuation marks into sound as we read a text out loud. Those sounds are comically physical in their guttural tongue-twisting nonsensical quality. The

In the open window there suddenly came light ● Beautiful Eleanor sat alone dreaming of but one thing ● ▬ Two years had passed ? since she met Sir Henry ● She would still remember the unhappy evening ? when her father had thrown him out ● They had been sitting in the park and Henry had said ● ‼ Darling ! Is this the first time you have loved ? ‼

Victor Borge
Phonetic punctuation | A Mozart opera

She had answered ● ‼ Yes ▬ but it is so wonderful ? that I hope it will not be the last ! ‼ ● Suddenly she heard a well-known sound ● It was he ● In two strides he was near her ? embraced ? kissed and caressed her ● ▬ ‼ Henry ! What is Love ? ‼ she asked ● He answered ● ‼ Well ? I could not live without

●●●●●●●●●●●● ● She asked ● ‼ Where have all

your thoughts been this while ? ‼ He answers ● ‼ With Thee ? my maiden

▬ ▬ ▬ ▬ ▬ ▬

Suddenly he was gone ● All she heard was the well-known sound of his departing horse

PHILIPS

Victor Borge makes a serious point.

full stop is a fart-like 'pbbbt' of the lips, the exclamation mark a 'pbbbt', preceded by a whistling sigh ('fffsss') to signal the vertical stroke above the dot. And it's not only Borge's voice that gives sound to content-less characters; it's his hands and face, too. Punching the air with his index stresses the 'pbbbt', an invisible line downwards accompanies 'fffsss', before being cut short by the jab of 'pbbbt'.

Borge's sketch is funny and clownish, but it gets at something rather serious: punctuation – all writing – comes to the reader as disembodied meaning, and as such is extremely vulnerable to misinterpretation. Without voice, we struggle to tell the tone. Without face or gesture, we have trouble identifying the emotion. That is why punctuation was invented in the first place: to make textual ambiguity less ambiguous. Digital writing is a special case, which we are still getting used to, lacking as it does the experiential dimension of touching the same paper as the letter-writer, and seeing their handwriting, and other human evidence such as crossed-out mistakes, pen smudges or vehement underlinings, offering clues to the state of feeling of their writer, and something of their human presence.

Studies have shown that we pick up social information less easily from digital writing than from handwriting. In one test, participants were offered brief written exchanges based on habitual daily situations ('would you like to have pizza tonight?'), including short one- or two-word answers, concluding with or without a full stop ('nope' or 'nope.'). Text messages with a full stop came across as less sincere, enthusiastic or warm, sometimes even as passive-aggressive. The same was not the case for handwritten notes. We don't expect end-punctuation in the informal medium of texting, so, when someone goes to the length of actually using some, we are startled, reading intentions into the extra effort, and deducing negative undertones.

There is something about handwriting that inscribes us. We are present. We have left our mark on a tangible object that we held in our capable hands, an object now held by the reader. Digi-talk, however, is the most extreme form of disembodiment, reducing the entirety of our animated selves into an artificial glyph floating in its insubstantial existence as a combination of electric impulses in the number soup of the digital ether.

We worry about this disembodiment. We worry about our tone, and about the other's. How will we be understood? How can we understand the other without their eyes laughing at our joke? Voice tone, gesticulating hands and wrinkles around the mouth are not add-ons of communication. They're intrinsic to it. And so we grasp at the stuff crowding around words to figure out graphically what we feel physically, and to translate those feelings into textually sendable objects: we use punctuation to represent a feeling (nobody could misunderstand !!!!!!!!!!!! for serenity), or images like gifs and emojis to convey moods, intentions and mini-summaries of, or commentaries on, our words. Sending a goodnight text, I might add a moon and star emoji. And yet, we're never satisfied. How would one catch that sudden honest eruption of belly-laughter? We need to upscale 'haha' into 'hahahahaha!!!', we try out 'lol', 'rofl', the laughing-tears emoji, or descriptive phrases such as 'literally cracking up right now'. We keep trying, because we crave conversation.

Not paying for number of characters and easy keyboard technology facilitate both minimalism (lack of paragraphs or full stops, even lack of words), and maximalism, effort-

'Roll your eyes' emojis. Samsung seems a bit confused.

lessly elongating letters, marks and images like chewing gum. Among all those puffers of emotion, tone and gesture, the exclamation mark stands out because it exists on all devices. You can't underline on your smartphone, but you can manipulate the look of a word. Calling up the emoji list and clicking yourself through is cumbersome on a laptop, but straightforward on a phone keyboard. Among the over-abundant wealth of emojis, however, picking the exact right one interrupts the spontaneity of words and feelings; iden-tifying it as reader becomes even harder and stalls that digitally induced flow. Among all glyphs, ! is most available, and most versatile, the most recognisable and most iconic.

— !!! —

Perhaps it's because ! is so boldly there, and unapologeti-cally itself, that people judge it as a marker of unwelcome excitability, of emotional exaggeration – and thus, inevita-bly, as a female thing. When the *Washington Post*, for example, first noticed Trump's ! habits, they introduced their observation with 'this chick needs to calm down'. Even supposedly neutral scientists can't help but reveal their bias when it comes to exploration of gendered speech habits: established linguists like Robin Lakoff consider tag questions ('isn't it?') and uptalk (when you end a statement with the upward intonation of a question?) as signs of lack of confidence in the speaker, not because there is evidence for any such lack, but because women tend to use them more often than men. In fact, studies have shown that question-taggers and uptalkers often occupy positions of power, and many of them are men. Those speech habits are less gender-specific than assumed, and certainly don't flag tentativeness. First and foremost, speakers use tag questions and uptalk for inclusion and friendliness. A kind of linguistic hug. And so with !.

In a 2006 study on exclamation mark use in two online communication platforms, linguistics scholar Carol Waseleski found that women exclaimed in 73 per cent of the 1,700 examined posts, nearly three times as much as men (27 per cent), confirming the assumption that ! is a mark of online female writing. But this was not because women are more excitable. Of all the ! messages, 32 per cent fell into the 'friendly' category – for example, 'Hello everyone!', 'I hope this helps!', 'See you there!' or 'Congratulations!'. Two-thirds of those friendly posts were written by women. Only 9 per cent of exclamation texts signposted strong emotions such over-effusiveness ('Thank you so very much!'), sneering ('Big deal!'), and aggression ('You stupid jerk!'). Of this handful of emotional posts, half were by women, half by men.

It's a myth that ! attaches to strong emotions only, and it's a myth that strong feeling in writing is a female preserve. Rather, women exclaim online for the same reason as they tag questions and uptalk in real life: they create a friendly space and supportive relationships. 'Hey, welcome!' is kinder than 'Hey, welcome.', particularly in the disembodied realm of cyberspace, where all that represents us is machine-produced squiggles.

Digital communication lacks presence, and so we use ! to negotiate tone and to add social glue. Shortly after

Waseleski's research entered the public domain, news of an extra Gmail function circulated, offering an 'emotional labour add-on': at the click of a button, the system would sprinkle your emails with ! or !!, or !!! where there were merely full stops before. Luckily (or not), this turned out to be a spoof, riffing on Waseleski's research with the aim of drawing attention to gendered perceptions of textual communication, and the crucial but undervalued nursing and maintenanace of social cohesion and connectedness performed by women.

— !!! —

! makes the web a warmer, more personalised space of belonging, and it also structures our visual perception of that space. In 2001, when the internet was taking its first steps into mass-media, the NNgroup consultancy issued guidelines for user-friendly homepages, suggesting the avoidance of ! at all costs ('chaotic and loud – don't yell at users'). The exclamation mark is a signal of importance, they acknowledged, but if it were used in that way on a home page the result would be a blizzard of !s, 'because all items on the home page should be of high importance'.

Two decades later, in the light of our web savviness, NNgroup now actually recommends ! in order to help users navigate a site. It's no longer the case that all items on the home page are of high importance. Crucial content needs to stand out, and the perfect eye-catcher is, of course, !. Or rather !!!. Employing eye-tracker technology, NNgroup discovered that three exclamation marks

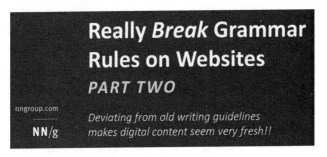

Really *Break* Grammar Rules on Websites

PART TWO

nngroup.com

NN/g

Deviating from old writing guidelines makes digital content seem very fresh!!

Look!! NNgroup reverses its rules!!

make the greatest impact on our attention, and create the least cognitive load. The eye easily confuses a single ! with the number 1 or the letter l. One the other hand, numerous marks confuse our eyes, and make our brains jump to counting, losing precious interaction time and bleeding cognitive energy. !!!!! – is it five or six? We can't help it. What a website needs to do is give users a comfortable navigation experience, providing just the right amount of difficulty, an intriguing but not-too-unfamiliar typeface, and a few visual and emotional peaks in the shape of !!! to help us manoeuvre and process what we're reading.

— !!! —

The internet is a particular form of awareness that affects us in a particular way. We've become used to it, but we're still figuring things out as we go along. We've imported our tried-and-trusted habits of reading and writing; and we're developing internet-specific kinds of engagement with text. And one another. Some of those engagements are cause for concern. Others bridge the gap of distance.

The exclamation mark has its foot in both camps, contributing to division and community, just as its shape contains both the circle and the line, the angular and the curve, focus and expansion. An electronic shout, paper surprise, admiration exploding on our diaphragms, multiplying in the cells of our vocal cords and erupting on our lips – there's nothing intrinsically good or bad about exclaiming.

! is what we make it.

EPILOGUE

Quo vadis!

In 2001 – long before people shifted their private lives onto the public domain of social media – Professor Naomi Baron predicted the future of English punctuation. She discerned three potential avenues: that 'punctuation will increasingly become a handmaiden to informal speech, following recent trends' (aka the internet, which Baron mentions just once); that punctuation will separate from speech, and signal syntactic structure only in written language; and that 'pointing will continue its centuries-old schizophrenia' of governing grammar as well as rhetoric.

Baron is an inspired linguist, but neither she nor anybody else could have foreseen the impact of digital communication on our lives, and thus on punctuation. Strangely, all three of her conjectures have come to pass. Social media and real-time texting have indeed lulled us into the illusion that we are speaking when we write. Adaptable as it is, punctuation has played the game in order to stay alive, morphing into emoticons and subtle mood informers which approximate the effect of tone of voice (that full stop in a dashed-off text that tells you the sender is maybe upset). Even as it binds voice into electronic communication, punctuation has also refocused on marking grammar, delegating to emojis some of its power to inform us about emotion.

Apart from those two seemingly contrary dynamics punctuation is experiencing in the digital world (punctuation clarifying grammar, and punctuation based on the pauses of speech), Baron's third assumption also holds sway: things continue as they have always done. Humans are creatures of habit and, rather than inventing a whole new way of communicating, we have mostly imported our old paper customs into the spheres of electronics. The internet is but a remediation of what we already have and do, just much much faster. The real revolution happened in Mesopotamia 6,000 years ago, when arbitrary scratches in clay represented arbitrary sounds referring to real things out there in the world. We're just improving minimally on that giant stroke of genius. Plus ça change.

— !!! —

Punctuation exploration has not stopped. The typographer collective of punctuation fan-boys and -girls called Progressive Punctuation is seeking to expand our current repertoire for greater nuance in electronic writing, with the goal to 'ending misunderstanding and misinterpretations once and for all'. Love, doubt, authority and (of course) irony all get their mark. Yet the self-declared 'movement' proposes no original signs, instead suggesting that we return to punctuation experiments that are already in existence, such as the infamous interrobang.

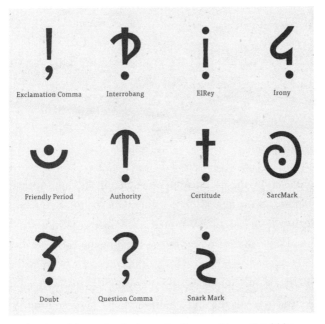

A selection of 'non-standard punctuation marks we should be using today', according to progressivepunctuation.com.

But there are also punctuation-obsessed designers who create completely novel glyphs. French typographer Thierry Fétiveau, for example, has developed eleven 'feelings signs', along with a new typeface called Andersen, in honour of Danish fairy-tale author Hans Christian Andersen. Working at a school before becoming a designer, Fétiveau noticed it was tricky to read out loud to the children and simultaneously perform the emotions

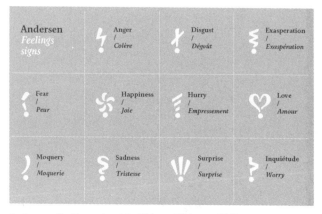

Andersen *Feelings signs*	Anger / *Colère*	Disgust / *Dégoût*	Exasperation / *Exaspération*
Fear / *Peur*	Happiness / *Joie*	Hurry / *Empressement*	Love / *Amour*
Moquery / *Moquerie*	Sadness / *Tristesse*	Surprise / *Surprise*	Inquiétude / *Worry*

Andersen 'feelings signs' by Thierry Fétiveau, 2018.

required by the narrative in an engaging and appropriate manner. Scouring children's stories for the most common feelings, such as anger, disgust, sadness, exasperation and joy, Fétiveau devised new marks embracing the start and end of the passage they refer to, thus preparing readers for the emotional pitch. All of his 'feelings signs' contain a central dot on the line, most of them representing an animated quivering zigzagging version of the exclamation mark, an unsurprising ancestor considering its staple task of indicating feelings.

Austrian designer Walter Bohatsch created a book, *Typojis*, to launch thirty new marks intended to alleviate glitches of communication. 'In our present era of "fake news"', Bohatsch asserts, 'renewed importance is being placed on statements' clarity and unambiguousness.' Punctuation can help us express what we really mean in writing when tone of voice, facial expressions and gestures are lacking. Bohatsch's choice of what to represent via glyphs is interesting: apart from feelings like outrage, contempt and disappointment, his set also includes more cognitive states like sagacity, tolerance and solidarity.

The typojis are not so much instructions for reading out loud, or indeed attuning oneself to the feelings expressed in a story, than meta-comments on the text, attaching to the end of the sentence they retrospectively qualify. Unlike emojis, the shape of the typojis are (true to their punctuation roots) abstract, although some bear some visual connection to the state of mind or feeling they are supposed to capture ('seduction', the fourth sign from the left on the last line, is appropriately curvy). The book is a beautiful piece of cooperative art, produced by designers, writers, philosophers and cultural historians. And the website allows for a curious animated superim-position of all signs: when the cursor hovers over the electronically stacked glyphs, out of the contours of the thirty unfilled forms emerges a black exclamation mark. ! is the matrix.

Typojis by Walter Bohatsch, 2017.

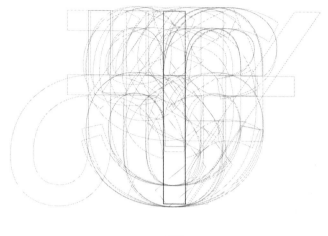

Bohatsch's exclamation mark as matrix.

Though Bohatsch uses typojis in his own communications, his project is essentially a not-so-serious artistic reflection on a practical and philosophical problem: how do we relate to one another in absence? What is being gained – what lost – when the 'I' that is thought, feeling, face, voice and hands becomes channelled into a small inky sign that is only a representation of me? Current punctuation explorations, like all punctuation across the thousands of years of its companionship with people, is a concerted though ever-dissolving attempt to capture what we truly mean. To hold it, store it, reproduce it, exactly as it originated in the head, or in the heart.

Our punctuation repertoire has been unchanged for nearly three hundred years. New signs, particularly those trying to catch and fix shape-shifting irony, have never been particularly welcome. It seems we're pretty satisfied with the signs we already use, so the most likely future of punctuation will be precisely the duality that Naomi Baron touches on – shimmering between grammatical assistant and voice imitator, refusing imprisonment in either.

So, are we stuck with a frustrating situation of forever falling short of being understood through our written words? Are we doomed to remain locked in mistranslation from speech to text?

We don't have to be.

⌣·!!!·⌣

Rules are neither good nor bad, but our attitude towards them make them so. In fact, they exist in order to help us experience, rather than shut down, aliveness. Grammar rules are not eternal or universal. They are historical, serving us at the moment with the particular technology at our disposal for a particular purpose. We outgrow them like clothes, and then we replace them. But we're still wearing something, we don't go fully naked. While the goal is not 'anything goes', rules don't mean much without respect to the intention of those inhabiting them, and it is foolish to impose inauthentic structures on living linguistic realities. Punishing anybody for an extra ! is historically inaccurate and ethically questionable. Whose rules anyway?

In her book, *Semicolon*, Cecilia Watson puts forward a beautiful understanding of rules, encouraging us to perceive them not as boundaries of the linguistically (and hence morally) right, but rather as 'outer limits of possibilities'. They are 'a framework within which to move'. They're not about correctness, but about effectiveness. Motive. Asking questions. An invitation to see how far we can stretch this, and still make sense. Can we tiptoe around the edge of nonsense, and still make knowledge together? Can we maybe even dance ecstatically in the exuberance of off-limit impossibility? At least, for the space that it takes to draw a vertical stroke, and a dot underneath.

A whimsical article in the 1901 *Boston Daily Globe* described punctuation as 'a gentle and unobtrusive art that has long been one of the misfortunes of man. For about three hundred years it has been harassing him, and bewildering him with its quiet contrariness, and no amount of usage seems to make him grow in familiarity.' While that is incontrovertibly true (witness the wealth of grammar guides still available), and while it's also true that punctuation is obstinately not going anywhere any time soon, it's anything but unobtrusive. It makes us do and feel stuff. It has punching power.

'Punctuation' comes from the Latin *punctum*, 'that which has been stung', as when we perforate paper with a pen when forcefully dotting the end of a sentence. Imagine now that this paper used to be animal skin in the Middle Ages. Imagine now that this skin is our skin, our eardrum, our retina, our nervous system. A well-placed exclamation mark penetrates the tender barriers of our being. It can give pain. Philosopher Peter Szendy proposes renaming punctuation as 'stigmatology', referring to the Greek word *stigma* for a mark, a tattoo, a blue bruise from pinching too hard. Punctuation is power, and it leaves traces on us. It jolts us into consciousness, and makes us experience experience. None other more than !. Maybe we can allow ourselves to surrender to its alchemy.

When Walter Bohatsch asked authors to contribute to his project, many refused, claiming they already had enough to do grappling with existent punctuation marks. Perhaps their rejection of tools that promise enhanced precision was also motivated by an unconscious enjoyment of that which is vague. Perhaps we actually revel in messy ambiguity. Perhaps we prefer it to the clean cold dish of the mathematically literal. Punctuation beckons us to tolerate anxiety, offering us opportunities to sit in uncomfortable confusion. As such it seems the antithesis to science, particularly the exclamation mark, whose ubiquity, catalysed by social media's addiction to it, asserts and reasserts again and again our human desire to feel honestly. Bohatsch's glyphs can, in fact, be seen as a form of antipunctuation, in that they reduce the play of ambiguity. We need punctuation to feel, but we don't want to be told too much about what those feelings should be.

Philosopher Paul Robinson finds the exclamation mark 'obviously too emphatic, too childish' – not in and of itself, but rather 'for our sophisticated ways'. In his satirical essay, he discerns a decline in question and exclamation marks in printed texts, a trend that betrays our distance from 'a sense of inquisitiveness and wonder that is distinctly unmodern'. Instead, he identifies an undue rise in semicolons and full stops, which 'imply a capacity for complex, dialectical formulations appropriate to our complex times.' But that's not praise. Far from it – such braininess cuts us off from our earthy humanity grounded in our capacity to be body, to be both mind and matter. Robinson suggests we acknowledge our 'emotional responses' to words and punctuation marks, and encourages us to develop not a set of rules but 'a set of feelings' towards each and every sign.

An Admirable Point is one such invitation to attune to those puzzling, powerful and playful shapes. Can punctuation solve problems of (mis)interpretation in texts? Can the exclamation mark save the world? Perhaps it can, and perhaps it doesn't have to. Perhaps it's enough if ! does what it was invented to do: attend to admiration; point out wonder.

Thanks!

Great thanks go to my editor Cecily Gayford at Profile Books who saw the project before I did, as well as Mark Ellingham and Jonathan Buckley for shaping the text into a book, and to Henry Iles for design, Nikky Twyman for proofreading and Bill Johncocks for the index, and Sam Johnson for the cover. Warm thanks also to my agent Max Edwards for his unfailing support, humour and kindness.

This book is one of the branches of the big old tree of punctuation on which I've been working, one way or another, for more than a decade. It all started with Sidney's brackets and the PhD that I was not writing, which kept me hooked on those little moons. Grateful thanks to my supervisors at Cambridge who taught me all I can do with words, particularly Hester, Raphael and Isobel. Thanks also to Professor David Crystal, who generously shared his thoughts on the transatlantic terminological difference between the exclamation mark and the exclamation point. My thanks also to designers Thierry Fétiveau and Walter Bohatsch for a conversation on new punctuation signs.

I wrote this book while working on my postdoc funded by the Leverhulme Trust and the University of Sheffield. My deep thanks to both institutions for allowing me unlimited time and freedom to research and write.

Warmest thanks to my long-term supporters, my late grandmother, and my sister Daisy, who both said I should 'just' write a book when I was still at school. Thanks also to my cousin Niloofar and my oldest friend Nele, both also long-term cheerers-on. Thanks to Joris for that naughty French ! term, and to Kim for proofreading, Meichi for building my website with me, Steven for authorly advice, Melanie for accompanying me on the way, Lisa for her kind patience in talking things through with me for so long, and JJ for helping me out of a particularly bothersome pickle.

My students have heard a lot (and maybe too much) about this book, but have always encouraged me, particularly Njomza, Emre, Sarah and Matt. I should also mention my dog Alfie, who, draped around my feet in winter, or snoring under my hammock in summer, kept me uncomplicated company in the somewhat individualistic task of writing a book.

I don't know how to even start thanking my two closest friends: Prem who invites me to feeling-writing when brain-writing has monopolised me for too long, and Siamak, my mirror, my Sufi fish-twin, who knows what it means to channel, and who knows everything else, too.

My last, best and deepest thanks to you who went with me to Ithaca and back after a considerable amount of time, and who gave me the most thoughtful gift, my website powered by green energy, that made me believe all this stuff about dots and dashes was worth putting out there in the first place. And so many things grew from that. My phone is full of photos of industrial towers for you, and I still don't know how Downton ends. Don't forget, habibi, that Icarus also flew. *Inta ya noor ayni.*

Images!

A book like *An Admirable Point* has an inevitable magpie aspect in its accumulation of images to illustrate points, exclamatory or otherwise. Every effort has been made to seek permission from image rights holders, but the author and publishers would welcome information in order to make good any absent acknowledgements in future editions.

We are grateful to Alamy Images for the photographs of European deputies holding ! (© Jean-Marc Loos); Amanda Gorman (© Media Punch); and Chekhov (© Süddeutsche Zeitung Photo). James Victoire for his motivational point. The Twitter photographer of *Last Christmas Wham!* and whoever first discovered and shared the ! shape of Yiland and Sican on the same platform. Adam Calhoun for his visualisation maps. Ben Blatt for his table. Image of Cynthia Nixon in *W;t* © Joan Marcus. The British Library for the Beowulf manuscript. Gerard Manley Hopkins' 'The Windhover' © The Bodleian Libraries, University of Oxford, MS Bridges 61, pp. 94-5. Richard Artschwager's *Exclamation Point* © ARS, NY and DACS, London 2022. Trump's wordmap was created by NBC. Progressive punctuation for their signs.

Renan Gross for the image from his blog 'Sarcastic Resonance'. Typeface design for the Andersen Feeling Signs © Thierry Fétiveau, Type Foundry 205tf. Walter Bohatsch for the typojis. The photo of H.W. Fowler © the Secretary to the Delegates of Oxford University Press.

Index!

Note: Italic page numbers indicate that relevant material appears only in an illustration on that page. Several books are discussed either as offering a source of guidance or as providing examples of remarkable punctuation. As some of the titles in the first group may be unfamiliar, all are gathered together under 'book titles'.

A

Absalom, Absalom!, by William Faulkner *52*, 82
'admiration (and detestation), point of' 22
Adorno, Theodor 113
Adults!!!: Smart!!! Shithammered!!! And Excited by Nothing!!!!!!! album 17
advertising, branding and logos 21, 49, 121
Alcanter de Brahm (Marcel Bernhardt) *58*, 59
Allen, Woody 119
Alpoleio da Urbisaglia, Iacopo 25, 27, 32, 39, 112
ambiguity
  attempts to banish 56–8, 145–6
  value of 55, 161
Andersen typeface 155–6
apostrophe 26
Arabic 45–6
art, an exclamation mark as 108–9
The Art of Punctuating, by Iacopo Alpoleio da Urbisaglia 25
Artschwager, Richard 109–11

Austen, Jane 55, 83–8
  use of exclamation marks 81
  use of semicolons 70, 83
authority, ! as a gesture of 113
authors' punctuation preferences 51, 76–7, 82–3, 100–1
Ay caramba! 55

B

'bangorrhea' 11
Baron, Naomi 153–4, 159
Bazin, Hervé 61
Beale, John 34–5
Beowulf 94–9, *96*
Bill of Rights, origin 10
biological nature of punctuation 102
Blatt, Ben 76–7, 81, 88–9
Blood Meridian, by Cormac McCarthy 51, *52*
Bohatsch, Walter 156, *157–8*, 158, 161
book titles
  Absalom, Absalom!, by William Faulkner *52*, 82
  The Art of Punctuating, by Iacopo Alpoleio da Urbisaglia 25

C

A NOTE ABOUT THE AUTHOR

Florence Hazrat is a writer and researcher from Germany, working on punctuation in language and culture, and on Renaissance literature. Before she discovered her secret passion for the exclamation point, she was a fellow at the University of Sheffield (U.K.) studying brackets in early modern literature, and at the University of Geneva (Switzerland), working on Shakespeare translations. Florence has been educated at the University of Cambridge and the University of St. Andrews where she has received her PhD on refrains in sixteenth-century poetry and drama. She is a BBC New Generation Thinker and the host of *Standing on Points*, a podcast about dots and dashes.

A NOTE ON THE TYPE

An Admirable Point has been set in Bodoni 72. To create this digital version of the type used by typographer, punch-cutter, and publisher Giambattista Bodoni (1740-1813), the International Typeface Corporation studied the Italian master's steel punches at the Museo Bodoniana in Parma, Italy and specimens from the *Manuale Tipografico*, a collection of Bodoni's work published by his widow in 1818. Bodoni 72 was released in 1994.